Brewster & Baldwin's Illustrated Catalogue of Carriages..

CATALOGUE OF CARRIAGES.

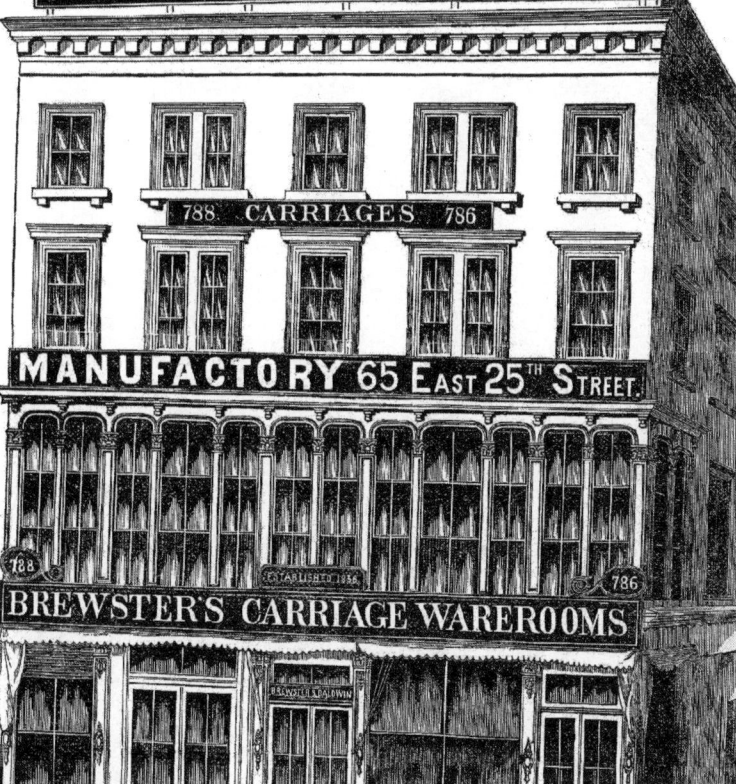

BREWSTER & BALDWIN'S Illustrated CATALOGUE —OF— CARRIAGES;

MANUFACTORY,

EAST TWENTY-FIFTH STREET,

NEAR THIRD AVENUE;

REPOSITORY,

786 BROADWAY, NEW YORK,

Next to Grace Church.

NEW YORK:
STONE & BARRON, STEAM BOOK AND JOB PRINTERS, No. 98 NASSAU STREET.
BETWEEN ANN AND FULTON STREETS.

Press of Stone & Barron,
No. 98 Nassau Street, between Fulton and Ann,
New York.

BREWSTER & BALDWIN, Established 1838.

TO PURCHASERS OF CARRIAGES.

In presenting to purchasers of Carriages this Catalogue as a guide in making their selections, the Subscribers would call their attention to the fact, that the Designs from which the Engravings are made were photographed directly upon the engraver's blocks from Carriages on sale in their Repository, and are therefore more carefully delineated than those ordinarily given upon charts; also to the fact that they have constantly on hand a stock of their celebrated

"BREWSTER WAGONS,"

of which they were the original builders, and which have attained such a world-wide celebrity.

In this connection they beg especially to call the attention of buyers to the fact that all **THEIR CARRIAGES**, as well as **THEIR BUGGIES**, are of **THE VERY BEST QUALITY, BOTH IN WORKMANSHIP AND MATERIAL**, and that they have no connection with the new concern of similar name on Fifth Avenue, who **Deal** in country-made Carriages. For this reason they request parties at a distance who may apply by Letter, to be very careful and address,

BREWSTER & BALDWIN,

New York, April, 1868.
786 BROADWAY.

Manufactory, No. 145 East Twenty-fifth Street.

BREWSTER y BALDWIN, Establecido el ano 1838.

A LOS

COMPRADORES DE CARRUAJES.

Los Subscriptores tienen el honor de poner en el conocimiento de los compradores de Carruajes, que este Catologo, es como guia para compras, y que los planes hecho sobre los zoquetes del Grabador, son laminas directa de los Carruajes que tienen en sus deposito para vender, y consequentemente dibujado con mas cuidado que sobre cartas ordinarias, que tienen tambien un surtido grande de

"CARROS CELEBRE DE BREWSTER,"

de cuales son los inventores primitivos, y cuales carros han obtenido una fama tan celebre.

En esta conexion piden especialmente la atencion de los compradores, a sus Carruajes y Buggies, cuales son de la mejor qualidad, trabajo, y material. Ellos tienen ninguna conexion en la casa del mismo nombre de la Quinta Avenida, quienes tratan en Carruajes hecho en el campo. Por esta razon piden a los partidos, de una distancia, de recurrir ò dirigir sus cartas a.

BREWSTER y BALDWIN,
Fabrica de Carruajes,

Nueva York, Avril de 1868.
No. 145 Calle Veinte Cinco, al Este.

SPOKES.

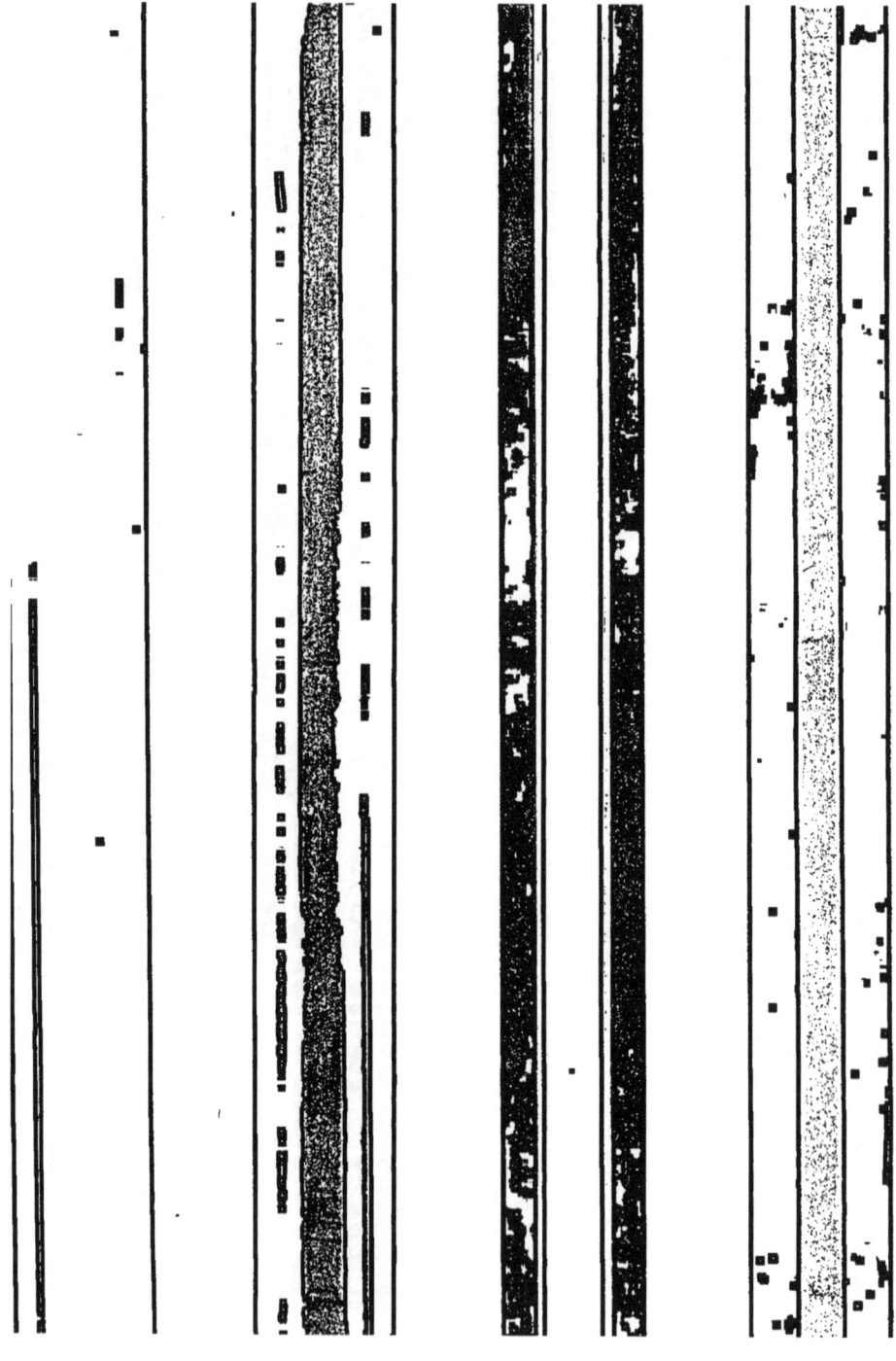

Brewster & Baldwin, 786 Broadway.

No. 701. $1400 to $1800, Gold.

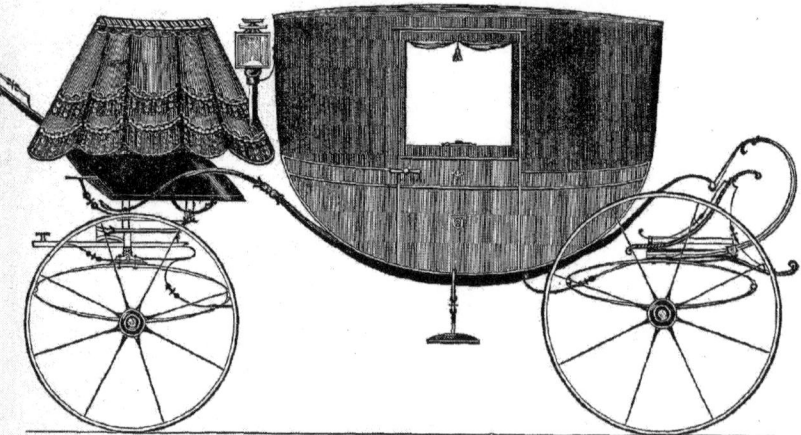

Elegant close-quartered Town Coach, with detached Hammer-cloth seat, over Salisbury boot, and standard behind for groom. Hung on C springs, over Eliptical.

Elegante Coche para la Ciudad, cuartos cerrado, con sillon aparte de paño de pescante sobre el pezebre de Salisbury y Estandarte para lacayo: suportado por resortes de C. y Eliptico.

No. 702. $1250 to $1600, Gold.

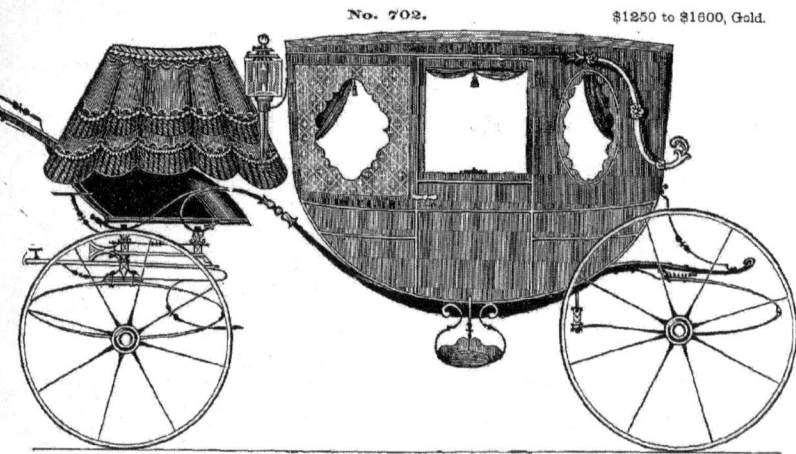

Elegant glass-quartered Town Coach, with detached Hammer-cloth seat over Salisbury boot. Hung on platform springs.

Elegante Coche para la Ciudad, cuartos de vidrio con sillon aparte de paño de pescante, sobre el pezebre de Salisbury: suportado por resortes de plataforma.

Brewster & Baldwin, 786 Broadway.

No. 703. $950 to $1250, Gold.

Fine close-quartered Town Coach, with French dickey-seat. Hung on C springs behind, over Eliptical.
Hermoso Coche para la Ciudad con sillon de Dickey : suportado detras por resortes de C. Sobre Eliptico.

No. 704. $950 to $1100, Gold.

Fine glass-quartered Town or Country Coach, very light, with French dickey-seat. Hung on C springs behind, over Eliptical.
Hermoso Coche para la Ciudad, ò el Campo, cuartos de vidrio, muy ligero, con sillon de Dickey Frances : suportado detras por resortes de C. Sobre Eliptico.

Brewster & Baldwin, 786 Broadway.

No. 705. $850 to $1100, Gold.

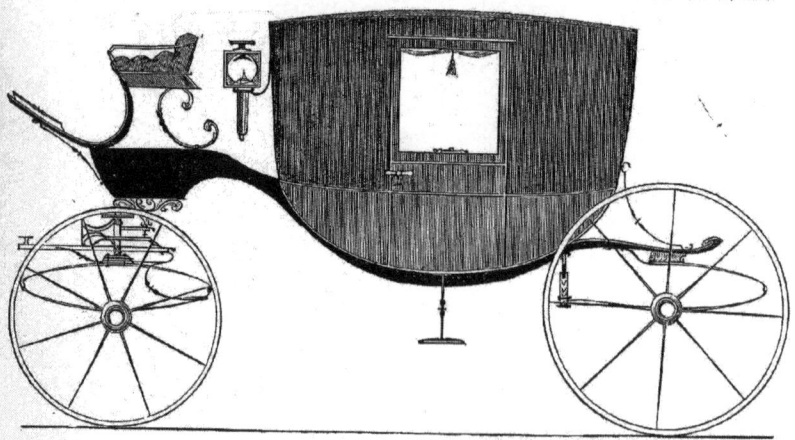

Fine close-quartered Town Coach, hung on Eliptical springs.
Hermoso Coche para la Ciudad, cuartos cerrado: suportado por resortes Eliptico.

No. 706. $850 to $1100, Gold.

Fine glass-quartered Town or Country Coach, very light. Hung on Eliptical springs.
Hermoso Coche para la Ciudad, ó el Campo, cuartos de vidrio, muy ligero: suportado por resortes Eliptico.

Brewster & Baldwin, 786 Broadway.

No. 707. $1050 to $1300, Gold.

New Orleans style glass-quartered Coach. Top opens, windows drop, French boot. Platform springs, richly mounted with silver.
Coche al estilo de Nueva Orleans, cuartos de vidrio, sombrero abierto, ventanas abiertas, pesebre Frances; resortes de plataforma; ricamente ornado de plata.

No. 708. $950 to $1250, Gold.

Fine glass-quartered Coach, Town or Country. French boot, windows open. Platform springs, very light.
Hermoso Coche para la ciudad ó el campo, cuartos de vidrio, pesebre Frances, ventanas abiertas, resortes de plataforma, muy ligero.

Brewster & Baldwin, 786 Broadway.

No. 709. $950 to $1200, Gold

Scroll-back, glass-quartered Town or Country Coach, on Eliptical springs. French boot
Coche ligero de ciudad ò de campo, cuartos de vidrio, rollo detras, pesebre Frances: sobre resortes Eliptico.

No. 710. $800 to $1200, Gold.

Scroll-front, glass-quarter, light Town or Country Coach. French boot.
Coche ligero para la ciudad ò el campo, cuartos de vidrio, pesebre Frances.

Brewster & Baldwin, 786 Broadway.

No. 711. $850 to $1200, Gold.

Paneled back-quarter, and movable glass front-quarter, light Town or Country Coach. On Eliptical springs.
Coche ligero para la ciudad ó el campo, cuartos detras de Albardon y los de frente de vidrio, morible sobre resortes Eliptico.

No. 712. $700 to $1000, Gold.

Southern coach, glass-quarters, very light; four Eliptical springs and perch; adapted to hard roads; hung high; very light; richly mounted with silver plate.
Coche del sur—cuartos de vidrio, muy ligero, cuatro resortes Eliptico y alcandara—Adaptado para caminos malos, muy alto—ricamento ornado de plata.

Brewster & Baldwin, 786 Broadway.

No. 713. $700 to $1000, Gold.

Crane-neck Southern Coach; glass-quarters; very light and stylish; suitable for the country or city. Hung on four springs and perch, richly mounted with silver plate.

Coche del sur—cuartos de vidrio—muy ligero y al estilo—conveniente para la ciudad ó el campo: Suportado por cuatro resortes Eliptico y alcandara, ricamente ornado de plata.

No. 714. $800 to $1100 Gold.

Scroll-back Southern Coach, glass quarters, very light; suitable for country or city. Hung on four Eliptical springs and perch, richly mounted with silver plate.

Coche del sur—rollo detras, cuartos de vidrio, muy ligero, conveniente para la ciudad ó el campo: Suportado por cuatro resortes Eliptico y alcandara, ricamente ornado de plata.

Brewster & Baldwin, 786 Broadway.

No. 715. $750 to $1050, Gold.

Curtain-quartered Coachee, with Hammer-cloth seat. Hung on leather braces. A very elegant carriage for the country.
Muy Elegante Coche, cuartos con cortinas, sillon dep año de pezcante, suportado por sopandos de cuero.

No. 716.   [$850 to $1200/.Gold.

New style curtain-quartered, light Coach, with French boot. Hung on platform springs.
Coche ligero de nuevo estilo, cuartos con cortinas, pesebre Frances: suportado por resortes de plataforma.

Brewster & Baldwin, 786 Broadway.

No. 717. $900 to $1250, Gold.

Glass-front Caleché (French style). Glass front is movable, and when removed is like No. 716. Quite light, and well adapted for both summer and winter, country and city. Hung on platform springs.

Caleche Frances, con vidrio en frente y movible parece al numero 716 muy ligero y acomodado para el invierno y el verano— Para la ciudad ó el campo: suportado por resortes de plataforma.

No. 718. $900 to $1250, Gold.

Same as No. 717, with a difference in the outline of the body.
Mismo que el No. 717, con una differencia en los contornos del cuerpo.

Brewster & Baldwin, 786 Broadway.

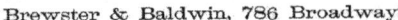

No. 719. $1050 to $1300, Gold.

Elegant glass-front Caleche (French style). Glass front is movable, and when removed is similar to No. 718. Has a leather fender at the front quarter. Is hung on Eliptical and C springs combined, making it elegant in appearance, and very easy to ride in.
Elegante Caleche Frances, vidrio al frente y movible, parece al No. 718, tiene un hallado de cuero a los cuartos de frente,—suportado por resortes de C y Eliptico, haciendolo Elegante y muy Dulce para andar.

No. 725. $800 to $1050, Gold.

New style low drivers' seat, quadrant-light Summer Coach. Very light, and very handsome, and very closely coupled. Hung on platform springs.
Coche ligero cuadrada para el verano, con sillon de cochero bajo, muy ligero, hermoso, y muy estrechamente juntado—suportado por resortes de plataforma.

Brewster & Baldwin, 786 Broadway.

No. 726. $800 to $1050, Gold.

New style, low drivers' seat, Summer Coach. Paneled back-quarter and glass front-quarter. Very light, very handsome, and closely coupled. Suitable for either town or country. Hung on platform springs.

Coche de asiento de cochero bajo para el verano cuartos detras de Albardon y los cuartos del frente de vidrio—muy ligero, muy hermoso y estrechamente juntado—conveniente para la ciudad ò el campo, suportado por resortes de plataforma.

No. 727. $800 to $1050, Gold.

New style, low drivers' seat, Summer Coach. Glasses in both quarters. Very light, very handsome, and closely coupled. Suitable for either town or country. Hung on platform springs.

Coche para el verano de nuevo estilo, cuartos de vidrio muy ligero, muy hermoso, y estrechamente juntado, conveniente para la ciudad ò el campo—suportado por resortes de plataforma.

Brewster & Baldwin, 786 Broadway.

No. 728. $800 to $1050, Gold.

Same exactly as No. 727, except that it has a leather curtain at front-quarter, which rolls up, and in winter is made warm by an inside pad.

Mismo que el No. 727, con la escepcion que tiene una cortina de cuero a los cuartos del frente la cual se puede doblar y en el invierno hacerse caliente con una haca dentro.

No. 729. $800 to $1050, Gold.

Same as last, except that it has leather curtains at both quarters, which roll up and make it very open for the summer, and with pads, which make it very warm in the winter.

Mismo que el anterior con la escepcion que tiene cortinas de cuero en los cuartos los cuales pueden doblarse abriandose para hacas por dentro.

Brewster & Baldwin, 786 Broadway.

No. 735. $2000, Gold.

Elegant eight-spring Chariot, with English boot, box step and perch. The most elegant dress carriage which is built.
Elegante Carrocin—con sillon aparte de paño de pescante sobre pesebre Ingles, Escalon de pescante y Alexandaras—El mas Elegante Carruaje echo.

No. 736. $1350 to $1550, Gold.

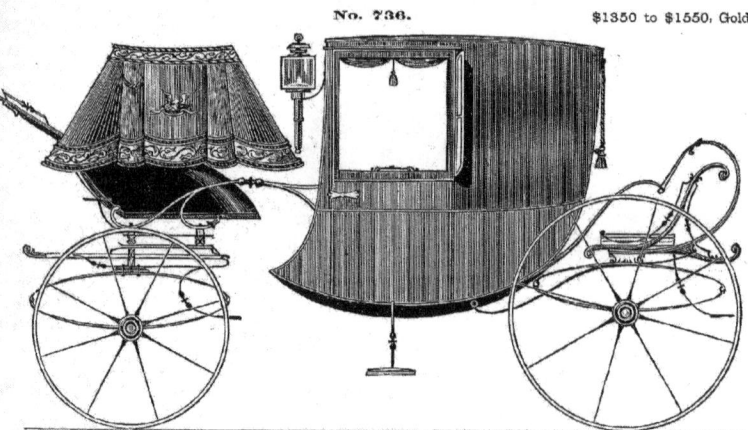

Elegant Chariot, with detached front. Hammer-cloth seat over the Salisbury boot. Hung on Eliptical and C springs combined, with standard behind.
Elegante Carrocin—con sillon aparte de paño de pescante sobre pesebre de Salisbury—con estandarte para lacayo, suportado por resortes de C y Eliptico.

Brewster & Baldwin, 786 Broadway.

No. 737. $1250 to $1450 Gold.

Elegant circular-front Chariot, with detached boot. English seat over the Salisbury boot. Hung on Eliptical and C springs combined.
Elegante Carrocin de frente circular, con sillon Ingles aparte sobre pesebre de Salisbury—suportado por resortes de C y Eliptico.

No. 738. $1200 to $1400, Gold.

Fine dress-Chariot, with French boot. Hung on Eliptical and C springs, combined.
Hermoso Carrocin pesebre Frances, suportado por resortes de C y Eliptico combinado.

Brewster & Baldwin, 786 Broadway.

No. 745. $1300 to $1600, Gold.

New style circular-front London Clarence. The newest and most elegant style in use. Hung on Eliptical and C springs, combined. Boot *de mode*.

Nuevo Estilo Clarencia de Londres, el mas Elegante y mas nuevo estilo en uso—pesebre de moda—suportado por resortes de C y Eliptico combinado.

No. 746. $1350 to $1600, Gold.

New style circular-front London Clarence. The newest and most elegant style now in use. Hung on Eliptical and C springs combined. Metropolitan boot. Box step.

Nuevo estilo de Clarencia de Londres, frente circular, el mas Elegante y nuevo estilo en uso—estando sobre resortes de C y Eliptico—pesebre Metropolitano—Escalon de pescante.

Brewster & Baldwin, 786 Broadway.

No. 747. $1300 to $1600, Gold.

Same as No. 746, except it has the ordinary step and French boot, and slight difference in outline.
El mismo que el No. 746 con la escepcion que tiene el escalon ordinario, pesebre Frances y pequeña, differencia en los conternos

No. 748. $1300 to $1600, Gold.

New style circular-front London Clarence. The newest and most elegant style now in use. Hung on Eliptical and C springs combined. French boot. Ordinary step.
Nuevo Estilo Clarencia de Londres, el mas Elegante y mas nuevo estilo en uso—pesebre Frances, Escalon ordinario—suportado por resortes de C y Eliptico combinado.

Brewster & Baldwin, 786 Broadway.

No. 749. $900 to $1250, Gold.

Three-quarter Clarence, circular-front. Hung on C and Eliptical springs, combined. Paneled boot. For one and two horses.

Clarencia de tres cuartos (¾) con frente circular, pesebre de Albardon por un ó dos caballos—sobre resortes de C y Eliptico combinado.

No. 750. $1200 to $1650, Gold.

Landaulet. A new style of circular-front carriage. Opens for summer use, as shown in No. 749. Is hung on Eliptical and C springs, combined. Box step.

Landaulet—un nuevo estilo de Carruaje, con frente circular, abierto para el verano, usado como en el No. 749, Escalon de pescante, sobre resortes de C y Eliptico combinado.

Brewster & Baldwin, 786 Broadway.

No. 751. $1200 to $1650, Gold.

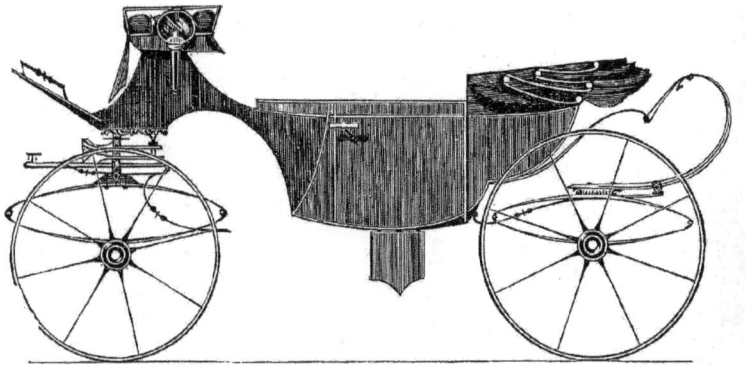

Same as No. 750. Shown open, for summer use. Closes, as No. 750, for winter use.

Mismo—abierto en el verano como el No. 750, y cerrado en el invierno como el No. 750.

No. 752. $900 to $1250, Gold.

Three-quarter London Clarence. Circular-front, neat, light, and elegant carriage for light horses. Hung on platform springs. A very desirable, useful, and elegant little carriage.

Clarencia de Londres tres cuartos (¾) con frente circular—bonito, ligero y Elegante Carruaje por caballo ligero—Suportado por resortes de plataforma, muy desirable—util y Elegante Carruaje pequeño.

Brewster & Baldwin, 786 Broadway.

No. 753. $800 to $1200, Gold.

Three-quarter, circular front, Coupé. Hung on platform springs. For one or two horses. Small seat folds down for children.
Coupé de tres cuartos, con frente circular; suportado por resortes de plataforma; por un ó dos caballos; pequeño asiento por niños.

No. 754. $900 to $1250, Gold

Three-quarter, circular-front, Coupé, with oval window in back-quarter. Accommodates two grown persons and two children. For one or two horses.
Coupé de tres cuartos (¾) con ventana oval in cuartos trasera, acomodation para dos personages grandes y dos niños—por un ó dos caballos.

Brewster & Baldwin, 786 Broadway.

No. 760.

Newest and latest style circular front Coupé. For one or two horses. Very light.

Nuevo y ultimo estilo circular frente; por un ó dos caballos—Muy ligero.

No. 761. $750 to $1050, Gold.

French Coupé, for one or two horses. Hung on platform springs.

Coupe Frances por un ó dos caballos—Suportado por resortes de plataforma.

Brewster & Baldwin, 786 Broadway.

No. 762. $750 to $1050, Gold.

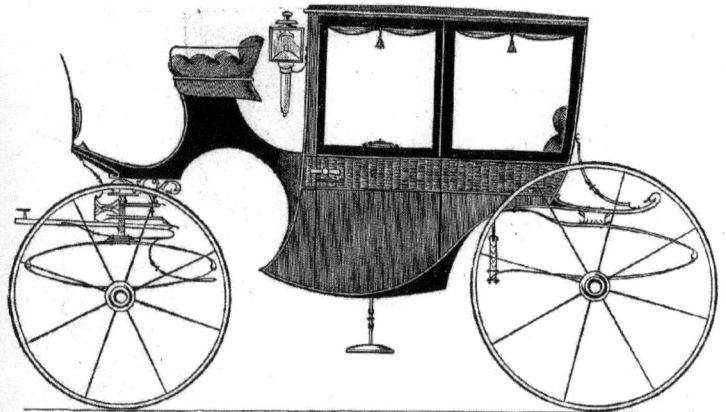

Straight front, new style, glass-quartered Coupé, for one or two horses. Hung on platform springs. Very light and airy.

Nuevo Estilo coupe, frente derecho, cuartos de vidrio, por un ó dos caballos—Suportado por resortes de plataforma, muy ligero y aéreo.

No. 763. $700 to $1000, Gold.

Ordinary style, straight front, French Coupé. Neat and plain. Hung on platform springs.

Estilo ordinario Coupe Frances; bonito y sencillo; suportado por resortes de plataforma.

Brewster & Baldwin, 786 Broadway.

No. 764. $750 to $1000, Gold.

French Coupé, for one horse; weighs 800 lbs. Hung on platform springs. An extremely light and very pretty carriage.

Coupe Frances, peso 800 libras, sumamente ligero y muy bonito carruaje; suportado por resortes de plataforma.

No. 765. $850 to $1250, Gold.

One-horse Landaulet; a new style of one-horse carriage, which may be thrown open in summer, as shown in No. 766. Hung on Eliptical springs.

Landaulet de un caballo. Un carruaje de nuevo estilo que se puede abrir en el verano, como en el No. 766; suportado por resortes Elipticos.

Brewster & Baldwin, 786 Broadway.

No. 766. $850 to $1250, Gold.

Same as No. 765. Shown open. In winter it may be closed up as No. 765.

Mismo que el No. 765; abierto en el invierno puede cerrarse como en el No. 765.

No. 770. $1250 to $1650, Gold.

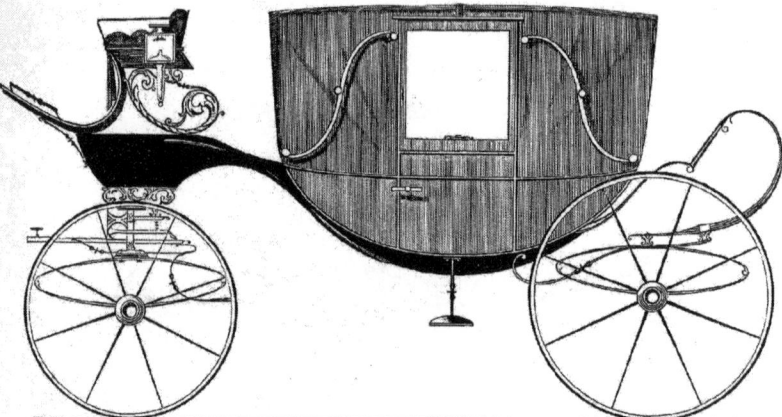

The Landau; a carriage long in use in Paris, but recently introduced by us in America. It is a perfect winter carriage; a perfect summer carriage, as shown in No. 771. Good weight for the city, and light enough for the country. Hung on platform and C springs, combined. French boot. The most popular carriage now in use.

Landau: un carruaje grande, usado in Paris, pero ultimamente introducido por nostros en America; es un carruaje perfecto en el invierno, como representado en el siguiente No. 771; buen peso para la ciudad y bastante ligero para el campo; pesebre Frances; el mas populo carruaje en uso; suportado por resortes de C y de plataforma, combinado.

Brewster & Baldwin, 786 Broadway.

No. 771. $1250 to $1650, Gold.

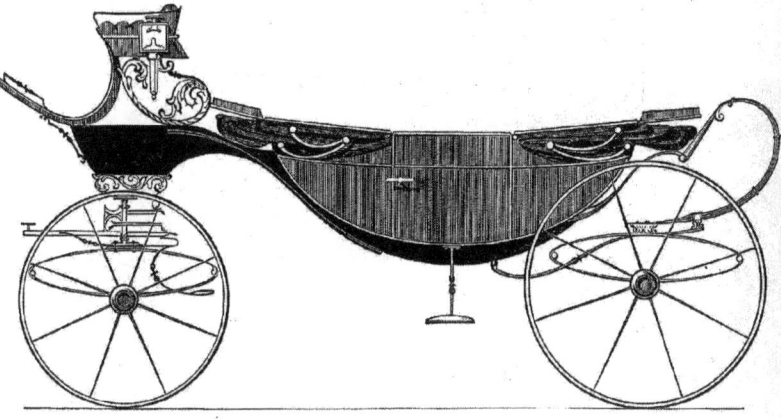

The Landau, shown as an open carriage. (See No. 770.)
Landau; como el No. 770; abierto para el verano.

No. 772. $1250 to $1650, Gold.

The Landau; a carriage long in use in Paris, but recently introduced by us in America. It is a perfect winter carriage; a perfect summer carriage, as shown in No. 773. Good weight for the city, and light enough for the country. Hung on platform and C springs combined. Boot *de mode*. The most popular carriage now in use.
Mismo que el No. 770.

Brewster & Baldwin, 786 Broadway.

No. 773. $1250 to $1650, Gold.

The Landau, shown as an open carriage. (See No. 772.)
Mismo que el No. 772.

No. 774. $1200 to $1600, Gold.

The Landau. On platform springs. Box step. Very light; weight not over 1,250 lbs. Suitable for either country or city, summer or winter. (See No. 775.)

Landau; conveniente para la Ciudad ó el Campo, escalon de pescante muy ligero; no pesa mas que 1250 libras; suportado por resortes de plataforma; para el invierno ó verano mismo que el No. 775.

Brewster & Baldwin, 786 Broadway.

No. 775. $1200 to $1600, Gold.

The Landau, shown as an open carriage. (See No. 774.)

Landau; un carruaje abierto mismo que el No. 774.

No. 776. $1200 to $1600, Gold.

The Landau. On platform springs. Box step. Very light; weight not over 1,250 lbs. Suitable for either country or city, summer or winter. (See No. 777.)

Mismo que el No. 777.

Brewster & Baldwin, 786 Broadway.

No. 777.　　　　　　$1200 to $1600; Gold.

The Landau, shown as an open carriage. (See No. 776.)

Mismo que el No. 776.

No. 780.　　　　　　$750 to $1100, Gold.

An elegant open Caléche, with detached front. English seat on Salisbury boot. Hung on Elliptical and C springs, combined. The most stylish Park carriage.

Caleche elegante y abierto; con separado frente, asiento Ingles sobre pesebre de Salisbury; suportado por resortes de C y Eliptico combinado; el carruaje mas al estilo para el parque.

Brewster & Baldwin, 786 Broadway.

No. 781. $800 to $1050, Gold.

Fine, round, open Caleché, with French front. Hung on Eliptical and C springs, combined. A very stylish carriage for Park use.

Caleche Hermoso, redondo y abierto con frente Frances, sobre resortes de C y Elíptico combinado; un carruaje muy al estilo para uso del parque.

No. 782. $1300 to $1600, Gold

Elegant eight-spring Caleché, with perch. Box step. The most elegant Brett we build.

Caleche elegante, de 8 resortes, con alcandara; escalon de pescante; al mas elegante Brett que hacemos.

Brewster & Baldwin, 786 Broadway.

No. 783. $800 to $1050, Gold.

Fine open Caleché, on Eliptical and C springs, combined; a neat and stylish park carriage.

Caleche Hermoso y abierto; sobre resortes de C y Eliptico combinado; un carruaje bonito y al estilo para el parque.

No. 784. $800 to $1050, Gold.

Fine round, open Caleché, on Eliptical and C springs, combined; a neat and stylish park carriage.

Caleche Hermoso redondo y abierto; sobre resortes de C y Eliptico combinado; un carruaje bonito y al estilo para el parque.

Brewster & Baldwin, 786 Broadway.

No. 785. $750 to $1000, Gold.

Fine, round, open Caleché, on platform springs; French boot.

Caleche Hermoso redondo abierto; sobre resortes de plataforma; pesebre Frances.

No. 786. $750 to $1000, Gold.

Fine, round, open Caleché, on platform springs. Boot *de mode*.

Caleche Hermoso, redondo y abierto; sobre resortes de plataforma; pesebre de moda.

Brewster & Baldwin, 786 Broadway.

No. 787. $800 to $1050, Gold.

New design of elegant open Caleché, on platform springs; fenders in front. Boot *de mode*.

Nuevo plan de Caleche; elegante y abierto; halladores en frente; pesebre de moda; sobre resortes de plataforma.

No. 788. $750 to $1000, Gold.

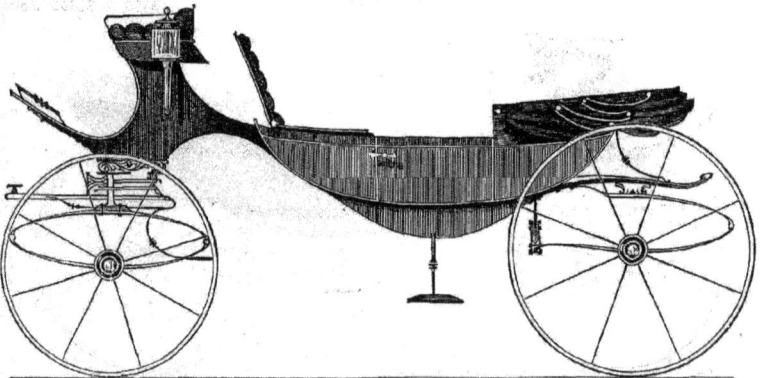

Fine open Caleché, on platform springs.

Caleche Hermoso y abierto; sobre resortes de plataforma.

Brewster & Baldwin, 786 Broadway.

No. 780. $750 to $1000, Gold.

New style Union Victoria Caleché, without door; fender over hind wheel; something new, very stylish; hung on platform springs.

Nuevo estilo Unido de Victoria Caleche; sin puerta; hallador sobre rueda tracera; una cosa nueva; muy al estilo; sobre resortes de plataforma.

No. 790. $750 to $1000, Gold.

The Otis Caleché; a light, new, and elegant open carriage.

Otis Caleche; un carruaje nuevo; ligero, elegante y abierto.

Brewster & Baldwin, 786 Broadway.

No. 791. $750 to $1000, Gold.

"The scroll back-quarter open Caleché," with French boot; new and very elegant design. Hung on platform springs.

Caleche cuartos tracera de rollo, con pesebre Frances; nuevo y elegante plan; sobre resortes de plataforma.

No. 792. $750 to $1000, Gold.

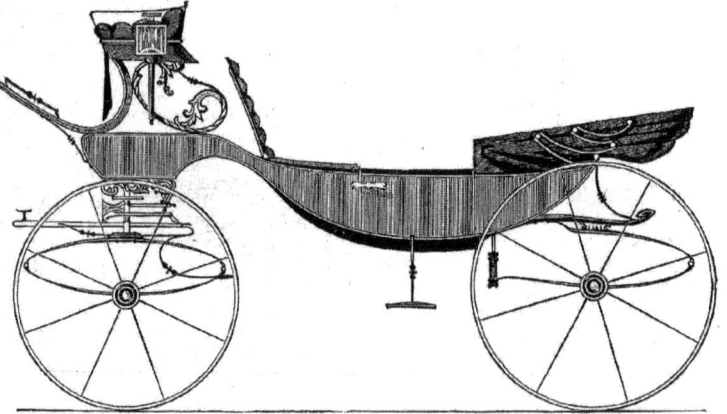

Binney Caleché; very light and stylish; French boot. Hung on platform springs.

Binney Caleche; muy ligero, muy al estilo; pesebre Frances; sobre resortes de plataforma.

Brewster & Baldwin, 786 Broadway.

No. 793. $850 to $1100, Gold.

Britzka Caleché. Hung on Elliptical and C springs, combined. The lightest and handsomest carriage now in use.

Britzka Caleche; sobre resortes de C y Eliptico combinado; el mas ligero y mas hermoso carruaje en uso.

No. 794. $750 to $1000, Gold.

Britzka Caleché; same as above, except that it is hung on platform springs, and is lighter; weight not over 800 lbs.

Britzka Caleche; mismo que el No. 793; con la escepcion que esta sobre resortes de plataforma y mas ligero; no pesa mas que 800 libras.

Brewster & Baldwin, 786 Broadway.

No. 795. $700 to $950, Gold.

Crane-neck Brett (Caleché); a light and stylish open carriage, very light, for the country. Hung on platform springs.
Pescuez de cigüeña Brett (Caleche); un carruaje ligero, abierto y al estilo, muy ligero para el campo; sobre resortes de plataforma.

No. 796. $650 to $900, Gold.

Crane-neck Brett (Caleché), second size; extremely light; especially adapted for sandy roads. Hung on Eliptical springs.
Pescuez de cigüeña, Brett (Caleche), secondo tomaño; sumamente ligero; especialmente adaptado por Camino Anenoso; sobre resortes Eliptico.

Brewster & Baldwin, 786 Broadway.

No. 797. $650 to $900, Gold.

The crane-neck Southern Brett (Calèche); side curtains of the hood movable; very light and stylish; richly mounted in silver. Hung on platform springs.

Pescuez de cigüeña, Brett (Caleche) del sur; cortinas al lado del sombrero, movible, muy ligero y al estilo, ricamente ornado de plata; sobre resortes de plataforma.

No. 798. $650 to $900, Gold.

Very neat and small Brett (Calèche); driver's seat low, so as to be driven by one of the family; weight, say 750 to 850 lbs. Hung on platform springs; a very favorite style for family use.

Muy bonito y pequeño Brett (Caleche), asiento de cochero pajo para que puede, ser conducido por un de familia; peso de 750 á 800 libras; un estilo muy favorito para el uso de familia; suportado sobre resortes de plataforma.

Brewster & Baldwin, 786 Broadway.

No. 799. $650 to $900, Gold.

The scroll back-quarter Brett (Caleché); low driver's seat, so as to be driven by one of the family; a light, roomy, and elegant carriage. Hung on platform springs. A very favorite style of carriage.

Brett (Caleche), cuartos detras de rollo; asiento de cochero bajo para que puede ser conducido por un de familla; un carruaje ligero y espacioso; estilo muy favorito; sobre resortes de plataforma.

No. 800. $650 to $900, Gold.

Light "Americaine" Brett or Caleché; very light weight; a new design. Hung on platform springs.

Ligero Brett (Caleche) Americano; muy ligero peso; un nuevo plan; sobre resortes de plataforma.

Brewster & Baldwin, 786 Broadway.

No. 801.　　　　　　　　　　$600 to $900, Gold.

The crane-neck Brett or Caleché; very light; hung on two springs and perch; side curtains of the hood movable; room for two grown persons and two children.

Pescuez de cigüeña Brett (Caleche); muy ligero; cortinas al lado del sombrero movible; lugar para dos personages grandes y dos niños; sobre dos resortes y alcandara.

No. 802.　　　　　　　　　　$600 to $900, Gold.

The scroll back-quarter crane-neck, paneled seat Brett; light; hung on two springs and perch; side curtains of hood movable; room for two grown persons and two children.

Pescuez de cigüeña Brett, cuartos detras de rollo, con asiento de Albarden, ligero, cortinas al lado del sombrero movible, lugar para dos grandes personages y dos niños; sobre dos resortes y alcandara.

Brewster & Baldwin, 786 Broadway.

BREWSTER & BALDWIN,
MANUFACTURERS OF
FIRST CLASS CARRIAGES,
786 BROADWAY,
[Next to Grace Church.] Cor. of T nth Street.
NEW YORK.

ILLUSTRATED CATALOGUES FURNISHED AT REQUEST.

LANTERN.   LADY PALMER.   BROWN DICK.   PRINCE JOHN.   NEW JERSEY.
FLORA TEMPLE.   FLATBUSH MARE.   LANCET.

Brewster & Baldwin, 786 Broadway.

No. 805. $800 to $1050, Gold.

Very light extension-top Caleché (Brett), with elegant French boot; top throws back at pleasure. Hung on platform springs. Especially adapted for the country.

Muy ligero Caleche (Brett), con sombrero de estension; pesebre Frances elegante; sombrero se baja a voluntad; especialmente adaptado por el campo; sobre resortes de plataforma.

No. 806. $800 to $1050, Gold.

Same as above, with different boot, and with sash-door.
Mismo que el No. 805, con differente pesebre y con puertas de vidriera.

Brewster & Baldwin, 786 Broadway.

No. 807. $800 to $1050, Gold.

Crane-neck, extension-top Caleché (Brett); very light and very handsome. Hung on platform springs.
Pescuez de cigüeña Caleche (Brett), con sombrero estencion, muy ligero y muy hermoso; sobre resortes de plataforma.

No. 808. $500 to $800, Gold.

Very light, six-passenger extension-top Brett; driver's seat low, so as to be driven by one of the family. Hung on two Elliptical springs and perch; may be used with one horse; pole and shafts.
Muy ligero Brett de seis passageros con sombrero de estencion; sillon de cochero bajo para que puede conducir un de familia; puede ser usado por un caballo; con lanza y flecha; sobre dos resortes Eliptico y alcandara.

Brewster & Baldwin, 786 Broadway.

No. 815. $1500 to $2500, Gold.

"Bracek *a 4 Chevaux*;" very stylish and elegant carriage for the races; has steps which fold down over front wheels, to enable a lady to mount driving-seat. Hung on platform springs, over Eliptical springs.

Bracek de cuatro caballos; muy elegante y al estilo; carruaje para careras; escalon doblando sobre rueda de fronte, para facilitar señores a subir en el asiento con el cochero; suportado por resortes de plataforma sobre Eliptico.

No. 816. $1000 to $1500, Gold.

Four-in-hand Phaeton, with rumble. Hung on platform springs. French boot.
Phaeton de cuatro asiento; pesebre Frances; sobre resortes de plataforma.

Brewster & Baldwin, 786 Broadway.

No. 817. $900 to $1300, Gold.

Six-passenger Park Phaeton; very light and very handsome. Hung on platform springs.
Phaeton de seis passageros, para el parque; muy ligero y muy hermoso; sobre resortes de plataforma.

No. 818. $900 to $1300, Gold.

New style "Canoe" Park Phaeton, combining the high Phaeton with the Brett. Hung on platform springs.
Nuevo estilo de canoa, Phaeton del parque; combinado, alto Phaeton con el Brett; sobre resortes de plataforma.

Brewster & Baldwin, 786 Broadway.

No. 819. $900 to $1200, Gold.

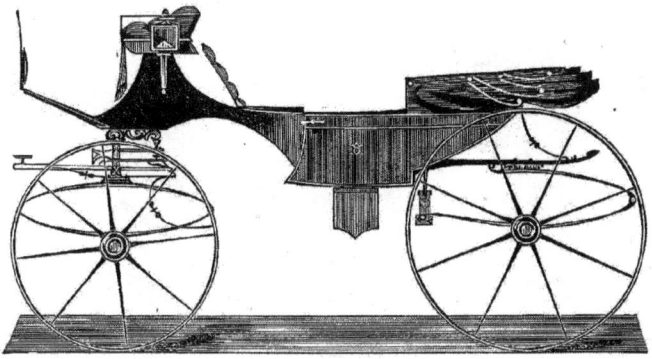

New style light Park Phaeton, combining the Phaeton with the Brett. Hung on platform springs. Box step.

Phaeton de parque; nuevo estilo ligero combinado, alto Phaeton, con el Brett; escalon de pescante; sobre resortes de plataforma.

No. 820. $900 to $1300, Gold.

Six-passenger Park Phaeton; new design, and very handsome. Hung on platform springs.

Phaeton de parque; para seis passageros; nuevo plan, muy hermoso; sobre resortes de plataforma.

Brewster & Baldwin, 786 Broadway.

No. 821. $900 to $1300, Gold.

Six-passenger Park Phaeton; round back; an entirely new design. Hung on scroll springs behind.

Phaeton de parque; para seis passageros, redondo por detras; un plan completamente nuevo; sobre resortes de rollo detras.

No. 822. $800 to $1200, Gold.

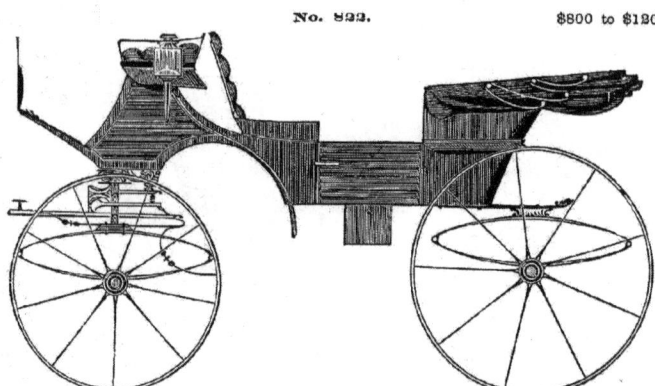

Six-passenger Park Phaeton, with imitation blinds on door and boot; box step; fenders on front-quarter. Hung on four Eliptical springs.

Phaeton de parque; puertas y pesebre sobre escalon, en imitacion del blindajes. Halladores en cuartos del frente; sobre cuatro resortes Eliptico.

Brewster & Baldwin, 786 Broadway.

No. 823.　　　　　　　　$800 to $1200, Gold.

Very light six-passenger Park Phaeton, with imitation blinds on boot; box step. Hung on four Eliptical springs.

Phaeton de parque, muy ligero, para seis passageros; pesebre en imitacion de blindajes; escalon de pescante; sobre cuatro resortes Eliptico.

No. 824.　　　　　　　　$700 to $1000, Gold.

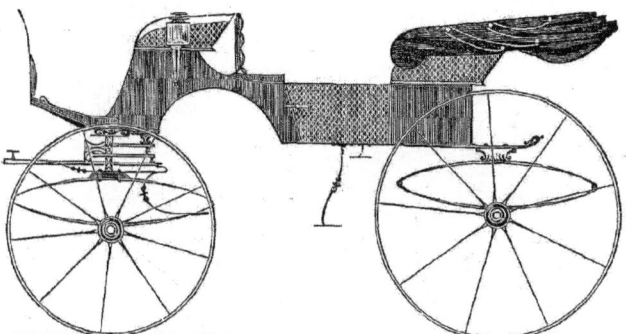

Very light six-passenger Park Phaeton, with imitation cane work; driver's seat low, so as to be driven by one of the family; the middle seat small for children; a light and elegant family carriage.

Phaeton de parque, muy ligero, para seis passageros; con asientos y puertas, en imitacion de caña; sillon de cochero bajo, para que puederser conducido por uno de familia; el asiento del medio pequeño para niños; un ligero carruaje de familia.

Brewster & Baldwin, 786 Broadway.

LANTERN.   LADY PALMER.   BROWN DICK.   PRINCE JOHN.   NEW JERSEY.
FLORA TEMPLE.   FLATBUSH MARE.   LANCET.

BREWSTER & BALDWIN,
MANUFACTURERS OF
FIRST CLASS CARRIAGES,
786 BROADWAY.
Next to Grace Church.]   Cor. of Tenth Street.
NEW YORK.

ILLUSTRATED CATALOGUES FURNISHED AT REQUEST.

Brewster & Baldwin, 786 Broadway.

No. 830. $700 to $850, Gold.

Very stylish four-passenger Park Phaeton, with imitation blinds on door; hood shifts to front seat at pleasure, like No. 836.

Phaeton de parque, muy al estilo; para cuatro passageros; puertas en imitacion de blindajes, el sombrero se muda hasta el sillon de frente a gusto, como el No. 836.

No. 831. $700 to $850, Gold.

Very stylish four-passenger Park Phaeton, with round back. Hung on four springs.

Phaeton de parque, muy al estilo, para cuatro passageros; redondo por detras, sobre cuatro resortes.

Brewster & Baldwin, 786 Broadway.

No. 832. $500 to $750, Gold.

Four-passenger Park Phaeton; panels carved from French wood; top shifts to front seat, as shown in No. 836. Hung on four Eliptical springs.

Phaeton de parque; para cuatro passageros; Albardon grabado de madera Frances, el sombrero se muda hasta el sillon de frente, como el No. 836; sobre cuatro resortes Eliptico.

No. 833. $600 to $850 Gold.

Elegant Mail Phaeton; hung on four Eliptical springs; top shifts to front seat, as shown in No. 836.

Elegante Phaeton de correo; el sombrero se muda hasta el sillon de frente, como en el No. 836; sobre cuatro resortes Eliptico.

Brewster & Baldwin, 786 Broadway.

No. 834. $600 to $850, Gold.

Elegant Kernochan Phaeton, with Stanhope pillar, front and back; a very light and elegant carriage for the park. Hung on four Eliptical springs; top shifts.

Elegante Phaeton de Kernochan, con coluna de Stanhope en frente y por detras; un carruaje muy ligero y elegante, para el parque; el sombrero se muda; sobre cuatro resortes Eliptico.

No. 835. $500 to $750, Gold.

Elm City Phaeton; very light, very roomy, and very stylish; top shifts forward, as shown in No. 836. Hung on four Eliptical springs.

Phaeton de ormo, para la ciudad; muy ligero, muy espacio y muy al estilo; el sombrero se muda de frente como en el No. 836; suportado por cuatro resortes Eliptico.

Brewster & Baldwin, 786 Broadway.

No. 836. $600 to $800, Gold.

Four-passenger Park Phaeton, shown with top shifted to front seat. Hung on four Eliptical springs.

Phaeton de parque, para cuatro passageros; el sombrero mudado al sillon de frente; suportado por cuatro resortes Eliptico.

No. 837. $500 to $700, Gold.

Light four-passenger one and two horse Park Phaeton; weighs about 500 lbs. Hung on four Eliptical springs.

Phaeton de parque, ligero, para cuatro passageros, de un ó dos caballos, cerca de 500 libres; suportado por cuatro resortes Eliptico.

Brewster & Baldwin, 786 Broadway.

No. 838. $500 to $700, Gold.

Adams Phaeton; the lightest four-passenger carriage we make. Hung on four Eliptical springs; top shifts, as shown in No. 836. Light enough for one horse.

Phaeton de Adam, el mas ligero carruaje que hacemos, para cuatro passageros; el sombrero se muda como el No. 836; bastante ligero, para un caballo; suportado por cuatro resortes Eliptico.

BREWSTER & BALDWIN,
MANUFACTURERS OF
FIRST CLASS CARRIAGES,
786 BROADWAY,
Next to Grace Church.]   Cor. of Tenth Street.
NEW YORK.

ILLUSTRATED CATALOGUES FURNISHED AT REQUEST.

Brewster & Baldwin, 786 Broadway.

No. 840. $400 to $600 Gold.

Leverich Phaeton, with cleft in side. Hung on two Eliptical springs and perch; very light; for one horse or two.

Phaeton de Leverich, con grieta por dentro; suportado por dos resortes Eliptico y Alcandara; muy ligero, para un ó dos caballos.

No. 841. $400 to $600, Gold.

Bowl Park Phaeton; very light and very stylish; for one or two horses. Hung on two Eliptical springs and perch. Top shifts to front seat, or takes off entirely.

Phaeton de parque de Borol; muy ligero y muy al estilo, para un ó dos caballos; el sombrero se muda al sillon de frente ó se quita completamente: suportado por resortes de Eliptico y Alcandara.

14

Brewster & Baldwin, 786 Broadway.

No. 845. $500 to $700, Gold.

Very elegant Dog-Cart; back seat adjustable, so that groom may ride back toward the driver. Hung on platform springs, over Eliptical. The most elegant and favorite style for the races.

Muy Elegante Carreton de Perro; il sillon detras puede ajustarse, de modo que personages grandes, pueden sentarse detras del cochero; suportado por resortes de plataforma sobre Elíptico; el mas elegante y estilo favorito para las careras.

No. 846. $525 to $625, Gold.

"Dog-Car de Chassé," with gun-case. Hung on platform springs. Blinds for ventilation.

Carreton de Perro, para casar; con caja de fusil; blindages para ventilacion; suportado por resortes de plataforma.

Brewster & Baldwin, 786 Broadway.

No. 847. $400 to $600, Gold.

English Dog-Cart. Hung on four Eliptical springs. Back seat folds in.

Carreton Ingles de Perro, asiento doblando por dentro; suportado por cuatro resortes Eliptico por detras.

No. 848. $500 to $600, Gold.

"Dog-Car de Chassé," with gun-case; back seat takes off and faces same as driver's seat at pleasure. Hung on four Eliptical springs

Carreton de Perro, para casar; con caja de fusil; asiento detras se quita y se pone de frente, como el asiento de cochero a voluntad; sobre cuatro resortes Eliptico.

Brewster & Baldwin, 786 Broadway.

No. 849. $450 to $600, Gold.

"Dog-Car de Chassé," with gun-case; back seat takes off and faces same as driver's seat at pleasure. Hung on four Eliptical springs.

Carreton de Perro, para casar; con caja de fusil; asiento detras se quita y se pone de frente, como el asiento de cochero a voluntad; suportado por cuatro resortes Eliptico.

No. 850. $400 to $500, Gold.

French Dog-Cart, with imitation cane sides. Hung on four Eliptical springs. A light and stylish tandem rig.

Carreton Frances de Perro, con imitacion de caña; ligero y de estilo, para caballos frente en frente; suportado por cuatro resortes Eliptico.

Brewster & Baldwin, 786 Broadway.

No. 851. $450 to $550, Gold.

New style drag-front Dog-Cart, with high driving seat; well adapted for tandem driving. Hung on four Eliptical springs.

Carreton de Perro; nuevo estilo, con asiento de cochero alto, muy bien adaptado para andar, con caballos frente en frente; suportado por cuatro resortes Eliptico.

No. 852. $450 to $550, Gold.

New style drag-front Dog-Cart, with high driving seat; well adapted for tandem driving. Back seat folds in. Hung on four Eliptical springs.

Carreton de Perro; nuevo estilo, frente bajo, con asiento de cochero alto, muy bien arreglado para caballos frente en frente, asiento detras doblando por dentro; suportado por cuatro resortes Eliptico.

Brewster & Baldwin, 786 Broadway.

No. 853. $400 to $550, Gold.

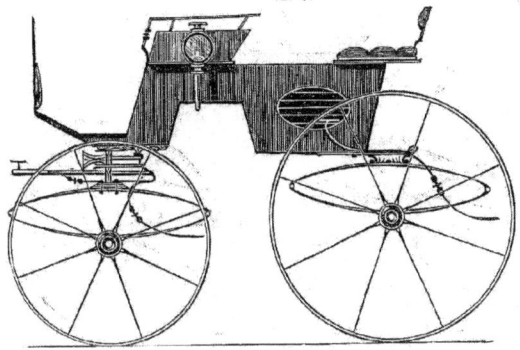

"Belmontina" Dog-Cart; back seat folds in; for one or two horses. Hung on four Eliptical springs.

Belmontana Carreton de Perro; asiento detras doblando por dentro, de un ó dos caballos; sobre cuatro resortes Eliptico.

No. 854. $400 to $550, Gold.

Planters' Dog-Cart Phaeton, with back seat to fold in. Hung on four Eliptical springs. A very light and elegant trap for one or two horses.

Carreton Factor de Perro, para campesino, con asiento detras doblando por dentro; sobre cuatro resortes Eliptico; un carruaje muy ligero y elegante, arreglado de un ó dos caballos.

Brewster & Baldwin, 786 Broadway.

No. 855. $400 to $550, Gold.

Very light "fold in back seat" Dog-Cart, for one or two horses, not heavier than a Buggy; very stylish. Hung on four Eliptical springs.

Carreton de Perro, muy ligero; asiento doblando detras, de un ó dos caballos; no pesa mas que un coche a dos ruedas; muy al estilo; sobre cuatro resortes Eliptico.

No. 856. $400 to $550, Gold.

New style light Dog-Cart; back seat folds in. Hung on four Eliptical springs. Pole and shafts.

Carreton de Perro; ligero y de nuevo estilo; asiento detras doblando; sobre cuatro resortes Eliptico, con lanza y flecha.

Browster & Baldwin, 786 Broadway.

No. 857. $350 to $450, Gold.

One-horse Dog-Cart; back seat folds in; very compact and closely coupled. Hung on four Eliptical springs.

Carreton de Perro de un caballo; asiento detras doblando; muy solido y estrechamente juntado; sobre cuatro resortes Eliptico.

No. 858. $375 to $475, Gold.

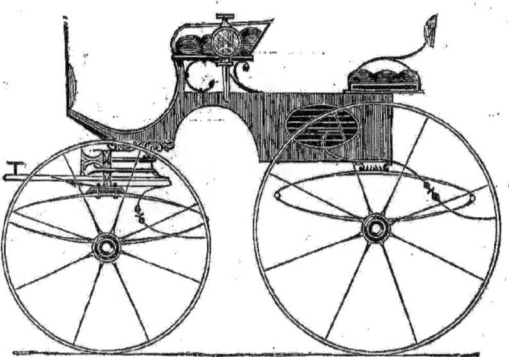

One-horse Dog-Cart; back seat folds in; very light and very compact. Hung on four Eliptical springs.

Carreton de Perro de un caballo; asiento detras doblando; muy ligero y muy solido; sobre cuatro resortes Eliptico.

Brewster & Baldwin, 786 Broadway.

No. 859. $450 to $550 Gold.

Russell Phaeton, for two horses. Hung on four Eliptical springs.

Faeton de Russell de dos caballos; sobre cuatro resortes Eliptico.

No. 860. $450 to $550, Gold.

Adams Phaeton, for two horses. Hung on four Eliptical springs. Suitable for fast driving.

Faeton de Adam, de dos caballos; sobre cuatro resortes Eliptico; conveniente para andar de priesa.

Brewster & Baldwin, 786 Broadway.

No. 865. $300 to $400, Gold.

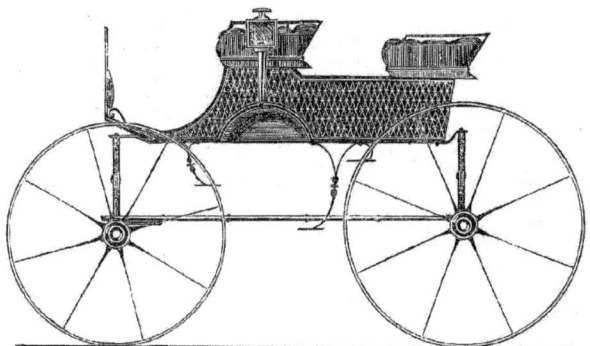

Elegant cane-side Bowl Phaeton, for one or two horses. Hung on two Eliptical springs and perch. A very light and beautiful carriage for the country.

Faeton de Bowl, elegante y lados de caña, de un ò dos caballos; suportado por 2 resortes Eliptico y alcandara; un carruaje muy ligero y hermoso para el campo.

No. 866. $250 to $350, Gold.

Farm Wagon, for one or two horses; back seat takes off at pleasure; tail-board lets down, so as to carry a trunk. Good plain wagon for depot use.

Carro de Arrendatario, de un ò dos caballos; asiento detras se quita a voluntad; la tabla detras se abre para admitir un baul; un carro muy sencillo para el uso de deposito.

Brewster & Baldwin, 786 Broadway.

No. 867. $300 to $400, Gold.

Cut-under, four-passenger, no top, high back wagon, for one or two horses. Hung on two springs and perch.

Carro cortado en frente muy alto, para cuatro passageros; sin sombrero ò tapa; de un ò dos caballos; suportado por dos resortes y alcandara.

No. 870. $300 to $350, Gold.

Light one-horse Bowl Dog-Cart; back seat folds in. Very compact, close coupled, and very stylish. Pole and shafts.

Carreton Bowl de Perro; ligero de un caballo; asiento detras doblando; muy solido; estrechamente juntado y muy de estilo; lanza y flecha.

Brewster & Baldwin, 786 Broadway.

No. 871. $300 to $350, Gold.

Light one-horse Griswold Buggy; back seat folds in. Hung on two springs and perch. As light as any ordinary one-horse Buggy.

Coche Buggy de Griswold; ligero para un caballo; asiento detras doblando por dentro; suportado por dos resortes y alcandara; tan ligero como cualquiera otro, coche de dos ruedas para un caballo.

No. 872. $275 to $350, Gold.

Light one-horse Copcutt Phaeton. Back seat for children. A very neat and tasty wagon. Pole and shafts. Back seat folds in. Hung on two Eliptical springs and perch.

Facton de Gorro; ligero para un caballo; asiento detras para niños; un carro muy lindo y a gusto; lanza y flecha; asiento detras doblando por dentro; suportado por dos resortes Eliptico y alcandara.

Brewster & Baldwin, 786 Broadway.

No. 873. $375 to $500, Gold.

Elegant "McKinney" Dog-Cart. Back seat accommodates two persons very comfortably, and folds away at pleasure. Hung on two springs and perch.

Carreton McKinney de Perro; elegante, asiento detras para dos personages grandes doblando a voluntad; suportado por dos resortes y alcandara.

No. 880. $450 to $550, Gold.

One-horse Dog-Cart, with top to take off. Back seat folds in. Hung on four Eliptical springs. A very elegant carriage. Pole and shafts.

Carreton de Perro de un caballo; sombrero se quita a voluntad; asiento detras doblando por dentro; suportado por cuatro resortes; un carruaje muy elegante; lanza y flecha.

Brewster & Baldwin, 786 Broadway.

No. 881. $400 to $500, Gold.

Bowl Buggy, with movable top and back seat to fold in; suitable for two light horses. Hung on four Eliptical springs.

Buggy Bowl; sombrero movible y asiento detras doblando por dentro; conveniente por dos caballos ligeros; suportado por cuatro resortes Eliptico.

No. 882. $450 to $550, Gold.

New style light cut-under Dog-Cart, with movable hood; back seat, which accommodates two persons very comfortably, folds in at pleasure. Pole and shafts.

Carreton de Perro ligero de nuevo estilo; cortado en frente con sombrero movible; asiento detras para dos personages; a gusto y doblando por dentro a voluntad; lanza y flecha.

Brewster & Baldwin, 786 Broadway.

No. 883. $450 to $550, Gold.

Very elegant Planters' Phaeton. Top takes off at pleasure; back seat folds in. Hung on four Eliptical springs.

Faeton elegante para arrendatario, el sombrero se quita a voluntad; asiento detras doblando por dentro; suportado por cuatro resortes Eliptico.

No. 890. $650 to $850 Gold.

New style Victoria, with round back. Small seat for children folds up. Fenders over front and hind wheels. Driven with either one or two horses.

Victoria nuevo estilo; redondo por detras; asiento para niños doblando por dentro; defensas en frente de ruedas detras, de un ó dos caballos.

Brewster & Baldwin, 786 Broadway.

No. 891. $700 to $900, Gold.

Elegant Victoria. Hung on Eliptical and C springs. Dickey seat takes off. For two horses. Full fenders over front and hind wheels.

Victoria elegante; suportado por resortes de C y Eliptico; asiento de Dickey se quita, de dos caballos; defensas completa sobre las ruedas de frente y detras.

No. 892. $700 to $900, Gold.

Elegant Victoria. Hung on Eliptical and C springs. French boot. Full fenders over both front and hind wheels. For two horses. A very light and elegant Park carriage.

Victoria elegante; suportado por resortes de C y Eliptico; pesebre Frances; defensas sobre las ruedas de frente y detras, de dos caballos; un carruaje muy ligero y elegante para el parque.

Brewster & Baldwin, 786 Broadway.

No. 893. $700 to $900, Gold.

McAllister Caleché, or Victoria. Room for two grown persons and two children; lid closes down over children's seat. Full fenders over front and hind wheels. Hung on platform springs. The handsomest light carriage in our stock.

Victoria ò Caleche McAlister; lugar para dos lacayos, personages y niños; el sombrero se baja hastas; el asiento de niños; defensas completa sobre ruedas de frente y detras; suportado por resortes de plataforma; un carruaje mas hermoso de nuestro Almacen.

No. 894. $800 to $1000. Gold.

Duplicate of No. 893, except that it is larger, and accommodates four grown persons.

Mismo que el No. 893, con la escepcion que es mas grande y puede acomodar cuatros personages grandes.

Brewster & Baldwin, 786 Broadway.

No. 895. $650 to $850, Gold.

Victoria, with narrow Dickey seat for one man, and may be moved behind, as shown in No. 896. Hung on four Eliptical springs. A light and elegant carriage for the Park.

Victoria con asiento angosto de Dickey para un hombre; se muda por detras, como en el No. 896; suportado por cuatro resortes Eliptico; un carruaje muy ligero y elegante para el parque.

No. 896. $650 to $850, Gold.

Same as No. 895, shown with Dickey seat behind.

Mismo que el No. 895; mostrado con asiento de Dickey detras.

Brewster & Baldwin, 786 Broadway.

No. 897. $500 to $750, Gold.

New style Miner Brett; low driver's seat, to be driven by one of the family. Room inside for two grown persons and two children. Pole and shafts.

Brett Minor, nuevo estilo; asiento de cochero bajo, para ser conducido por un de familla; lugar por dentro para dos personajes grandes y dos niños; lanza y flecha.

No. 898. $750 to $900, Gold.

New style elegant Victoria; full fenders. Hung on platform springs. Imitation cane sides. A very elegant and new design. Pole and shafts.

Victoria elegante y de nuevo estilo; defensas completa; suportado por resortes de plataforma; lades imitacion de caña; un y elegante muy nuevo plan; con lanza y flecha.

Brewster & Baldwin, 786 Broadway.

No. 899. $750 to $900, Gold.

Very fine Victoria, with Metropolitan boot. Imitation cane side. Full fenders. Hung low, and on four Elliptical springs. Pole and shafts.

Victoria muy hermoso, con pesebre Metropolitano; lados imitacion de caña; defensas completa; suportado por cuatro resortes Eliptico, y muy bajo, con lanza y flecha.

No. 900. $700 to $850, Gold.

New style round end, cane-side Victoria. Full fenders. Platform springs. Small seat for children, to fold in. Light enough for one horse. Pole and shafts.

Victoria, punta redonda; nuevo estilo, lados de caña; defensas completa; resortes de plataforma; asiento pequeño para niños doblando por dentro; bastante ligero para un caballo; con lanza y flecha.

Brewster & Baldwin, 786 Broadway.

No. 901. $650 to $800, Gold.

New style round end, plain side Victoria. Full fenders. Platform springs. Small seat for children folds out. Light enough for one horse. Pole and shafts.

Victoria, punta redonda; nuevo estilo, lados sencillo; defensas completa; resortes de plataforma; asiento pequeño para niños doblando por dentro; bastante ligero para un caballo; con lanza y flecha.

No. 902. $600 to $750, Gold.

"Victoria Mylord." Child's seat folds in. Full fenders. Platform springs. Light enough for one horse. Pole and shafts.

Victoria "Mylord;" asiento para niño doblando; defensas completa; resortes de plataforma; bastante ligero para un caballo; con lanza y flecha.

Brewster & Baldwin, 786 Broadway.

No. 903. $450 to $600, Gold.

One-horse Cabriolet Victoria. Hung on platform springs. Hung low, and easy of access. Fenders over hind wheels. Very light, very genteel, and very comfortable.

Victoria Cabriolete de un caballo; suportado por resortes de plataforma; bajo y facil de acceso; defensas sobre ruedas detras; muy ligero y agradable.

No. 904. $475 to $625, Gold.

Same as No. 903, with full fenders and a shade heavier; for one or two horses.

Mismo que el No. 903; con defensas completa y un poco mas pesado para un ó dos caballos.

Brewster & Baldwin, 786 Broadway.

No. 905. $450 to $600 Gold.

Very light one-horse Victoria. Fenders over hind wheels. Hung on platform springs. Easy of access, very low swung, very light, and very handsome. Pole and shafts.

Victoria, muy ligero de un caballo; defensas sobre ruedas detras; suportado por resortes de plataforma; facil de acceso; muy bajo, muy ligero, y muy hermoso; con lanza y flecha.

No. 906. $400 to $550. Gold.

One-horse Victoria Cabriolet. Hung on two springs and perch. Fenders over hind wheels. Pole and shafts.

Victoria Cabriolete de un caballo; suportado por dos resortes y alcandara; defensas sobre ruedas detras; con lanza y flecha.

Brewster & Baldwin, 786 Broadway.

No. 907. $400 to $550, Gold.

Very light and elegant one-horse Victoria Cabriolet, on two springs and perch. Fenders over hind wheels. Pole and shafts. Victoria, for pair of horses.

Victoria Cabriolete ; muy ligero y elegante, para un caballo ; sobre dos resortes y alcandara ; defensas sobre ruedas detras ; con lanza y flecha.

No. 908.

Victoria, with pair of horses.

Victoria de dos caballos.

Brewster & Baldwin, 786 Broadway.

No. 920. $350 to $450, Gold.

Very light one-horse five-passenger Rockaway, suitable for the country. Pole and shafts. Hung on two Eliptical springs and perch.
Rockaway, muy ligero, para cinco passageros, de un caballo; conveniente por el campo; con lanza y flecha; suportado por dos resortes Eliptico y alcandara.

No. 921. $350 to $500, Gold.

Six-seat Ambulance, with baggage-rack, suitable for depot use. Hung on two Eliptical springs, with perch.
Ambulante, sies asientos, con caja para equipage; conveniente para un deposito; suportado por resortes Eliptico y alcandara.

Brewster & Baldwin, 786 Broadway.

No. 922. $350 to $400, Gold.

Light Germantown Rockaway, for one or two horses; driver's seat takes away, and a leather dash inserted, which makes a light four-passenger carriage for one horse. Hung on two springs and porch. A very suitable carriage for the country.
Rockaway Alemania, de un ò dos caballos, ligero; asiento de cochero se quita y se pone, cinturon de cuero; un carruaje ligero para cuatro passajeros de un caballo; suportado por dos resortes y alcandara; muy ligero, conveniente para el campo.

No. 923. $600 to $750, Gold.

Six-passenger, sash-door, cut-under Germantown Rockaway. The most desirable country carriage built, being very light.
Rockaway Alemania, para seis passageros; con puerta de vidriera; cortado en frente para ruedas; un carruaje echo a proposito para el campo y muy ligero.

Brewster & Baldwin, 786 Broadway.

No. 924. $550 to $700, Gold.

Very light and very elegant low-door, six-passenger, O. G. back Germantown Rockaway; wheels cut under. Hung on two springs and perch. Belt of imitation cane-work. Leather curtains at sides and back.
Rockaway Alemania, para seis passageros; muy ligero y muy elegante; puerta baja; O. G. por detras, cortado para ruedas de frente; suportado por dos resortes y alcandara; trabajo al rededor con imitacion de caña; cortinas de cuero por los lados y por detras.

No. 925. $625 to $775, Gold.

Very light and very elegant high-door, six-passenger, O. G. back Germantown Rockaway; wheels cut under. Hung on two Eliptical springs and perch. Belt of carved French wood. Leather curtains at sides and back.
Rockaway Alemania, muy ligero y muy elegante; puerta alta, para seis passageros; O. G. por detras cortado para ruedas de frente; suportado por dos resortes y alcandara; cinturon de modera Frances grabado, cortinas de cuero por los lados y por detras.

Brewster & Baldwin, 786 Broadway.

No. 926. $750 to $900, Gold.

Six-passenger, sash-door Germantown Rockaway; wheels cut under. Hung on platform springs. Leather curtains at sides, and paddings for winter use; driver's seat is separated by a movable division, with two glasses to drop; back is paneled, with one window to drop. The most convenient family carriage made.

Rockaway Alemania; puerta de vidriera, para seis passageros; cortado para ruedas de frente; suportado por resortes de plataforma; cortinas de cuero por los lados y ventanas para el invierno; asiento de cochero movible por una division con una ventana de vidrio bajando; Albardon por detras, con una ventana bajando; un carruaje de familia, muy conveniente por la echadura.

No. 927. $750 to $900 Gold.

Six-passenger, sash-door Germantown Rockaway; wheels cut under. Hung on platform springs. Leather curtains at sides; driver's seat is separated by a movable partition, with two glasses to drop; curtain behind; a light, neat, country carriage.

Rockaway Alemania, puerta de vidriera, para seis passageros; cortada en frente para ruedas; suportado por resortes de plataforma; cortinas de cuero por los lados; asiento de cochero movible por una particion, con dos ventanas de vidrio bajando; un carruaje lindo y ligero para el campo, cortinas detras.

Brewster & Baldwin, 786 Broadway.

No. 928.　　　　　　　　　　　　　　　　　　　　　　$700 to $850, Gold.

Very light, new pattern, sash-door Elm City Rockaway; O. G. back; belt of imitation cane-work; leather curtains sides and back. Hung on platform springs. Splendid carriage for the country, and for a gentleman's own driving.

Rockaway de la cuidad de Elm; muy ligero, nuevo modo de vidriera, O. G. por detras; cinturon imitacion de caña; cortinas de cuero por los lados y por detras; suportado por resortes de plataforma; un carruaje esplendido para el campo, y por un señor conducir.

No. 929.　　　　　　　　　　　　　　　　　　　　　　$650 to $850, Gold.

Six-passenger, sash-door Germantown Rockaway; wheels cut under. Hung on platform springs. Leather curtains at sides, and paddings for winter use; driver's seat is separated by a movable division, with two glasses to drop; back is paneled, with one window to drop. A most desirable family carriage.

Rockaway Alemania, puertas de vidriera, para seis pasajeros; cortado para ruedas de frente; suportado por resortes de plataforma; cortinas de cuero por los lados y ventana para el invierno; asiento de cochero movible por una division con dos vidrios bajando; albardon por detras con ventana bajando; un carruaje muy excelente de familia.

Brewster & Baldwin, 786 Broadway.

No. 930. $750 to $900, Gold.

Six-passenger, sash-door Germantown Rockaway; O. G. back; wheels cut under. Hung on four Elliptical springs. Leather curtains at sides, and paddings for winter use; belt rail of carved French wood; driver's seat is separated by a movable division, with two glasses to drop; back is paneled, with one window to drop; silk curtains to all windows. An elegant family carriage.

Rockaway Alemania, puerta de vidriera, para seis pasajeros; O. G. por detras; cortado para ruedas de frente; suportado por resortes Elíptico; cortinas de cuero por los lados y ventana; para el invierno; cinturon al rededor de madera Francés grabado; asiento de cochero movible por una division con dos vidrios bajando; albardon por detras con una ventana bajando; cortinas de seda á todas las ventanas; un carruaje elegante para familia.

No. 931. $800 to $950, Gold.

Six-passenger, sash-door, Germantown Rockaway; wheels cut under. Hung on platform springs. Oval window in back-quarter; curtain and pad at the front-quarter; paneled behind, with window to drop; driver's seat is separated by a movable partition, with two glasses in it to drop; silk curtains to all windows. Very desirable family carriage. Either for town or country.

Rockaway Alemania, puerta de vidriera, para seis pasajeros; cortado por do frente; suportado por resortes de plataforma; ventana oval en los cuartos por detras; albarcion detras con ventana bajando; asiento de cochero movible por una particion con dos vidrios bajando; cortinas de seda á todas las ventanas; muy conveniente carruaje de familia; para la ciudad o el campo.

Brewster & Baldwin, 786 Broadway.

No. 932. $800 to $950, Gold.

Elegant Rockaway Coach, for six passengers, including driver. Sash door; oval glass in back-quarter; square glass in front-quarter, which is movable in summer; division front, with two glasses to drop, separate the driver from those inside; panel behind, with one window to drop; silk curtains at all windows. Hung on platform springs. A very graceful and useful family carriage.

Rockaway coche elegante, puerta de vidriera; vidrio oval detras; vidrio cuadrado en frente el cual es movible en el verano por una division con dos vidrios bajando; asiento de cochero aparte de los por dentro; albardon por detras con una ventana bajando; cortinas de seda á todos las ventanas; suportado por resortes de plataforma; un carruaje muy gracioso y util para familia.

No. 933. $800 to $950, Gold.

New style and very elegant Elm City cut-under, six-passenger, Rockaway Coach; O. G. back; oval light in back-quarter; square glass in front-quarter, which is movable for summer use; belt French carved wood; driver's seat is separated by a movable division, with two glasses to open; back is paneled, with one window to open or drop; silk curtains to all windows. A very nice family carriage.

Rockaway coche de nuevo estilo y muy elegante de la ciudad de Elm, para seis pasajeros; cortado para rueda de frente; O. G. por detras; oval en cuartos detras; vidrio cuadrada en frente el cual es movible para uso en el verano; cinturon de madera Frances grabado; asiento de cochero aparte y movible por una division con dos vidrios abiertos; albardon por detras, con una ventana bajando o abierto; cortinas de seda á todos las ventanas; un carruaje muy lindo de familia.

Brewster & Baldwin, 786 Broadway.

No. 934. $800 to $950, Gold.

New pattern and elegant Rockaway Coach, for six persons, including driver; sash door; oval window in back-quarter; square window in front-quarter, which is movable in summer. Hung on platform springs. Driver's seat is separated by a movable partition, with two windows in it to drop; back is paneled, with one window to drop; driver is always protected from the weather.

Rockaway coche; nuevo modo y elegante para seis passageros y cochero incluido; puerta de vidriera; ventana oval detras; ventana cuadrada en frente movible en el verano; suportado por resortes de plataforma; asiento de cochero aparte y movible por una particion con dos ventanas bajando; albardon detras, con una ventana bajando; el cochero esta siempre a cobierto del tiempo.

No. 940. $800 to $1000, Gold.

Low seat, new style, curtain-quarter Rockaway Coach; paneled back and front, with windows to drop; curtain sides, with paddings for winter use. The lightest and handsomest country carriage in our stock. Hung on platform springs.

Rockaway coche; asiento bajo, **nuevo** estilo; cortinas en los cuartos; albardon detras y frente con ventanas bajando; cortinas por los lados con ventanas para el invierno; el carruaje mas ligero y mas hermoso para el campo que tenemos; suportado por resortes de plataforma

Brewster & Baldwin, 786 Broadway.

No. 941. $800 to $1000, Gold.

High driving-seat, curtain-quarter Coach; paneled back and front, with window to drop; curtain sides, with paddings for winter use. Hung on platform springs.
Coche con asiento de cochero alto, cuartos con cortinas; albardon en frente y detras con ventana bajando; cortinas por los lados con ventanas para el invierno; suportado por resortes de plataforma.

No. 942. $800 to $1000, Gold.

New pattern curtain-quarter Rockaway Coach, with high driver's seat; imitation blinds in door. Hung on platform springs. A light and very stylish carriage for summer and winter, city and country use.
Rockaway coche, nuevo modo; cuartos con cortinas; asiento de cochero alto; imitacion de blindajes en puerta; suportado por resortes de plataforma; un carruaje muy ligero y muy al estilo para el verano y el invierno; de ciudad ó campo.

Brewster & Baldwin, 786 Broadway.

LANTERN.   LADY PALMER.   BROWN DICK.   PRINCE JOHN.   NEW JERSEY.
  FLORA TEMPLE.   FLATBUSH MARE.   LANCET.

BREWSTER & BALDWIN,
MANUFACTURERS OF
FIRST CLASS CARRIAGES,
786 BROADWAY,
Next to Grace Church.]   Cor. of Tenth Street.
NEW YORK.

ILLUSTRATED CATALOGUES FURNISHED AT REQUEST.

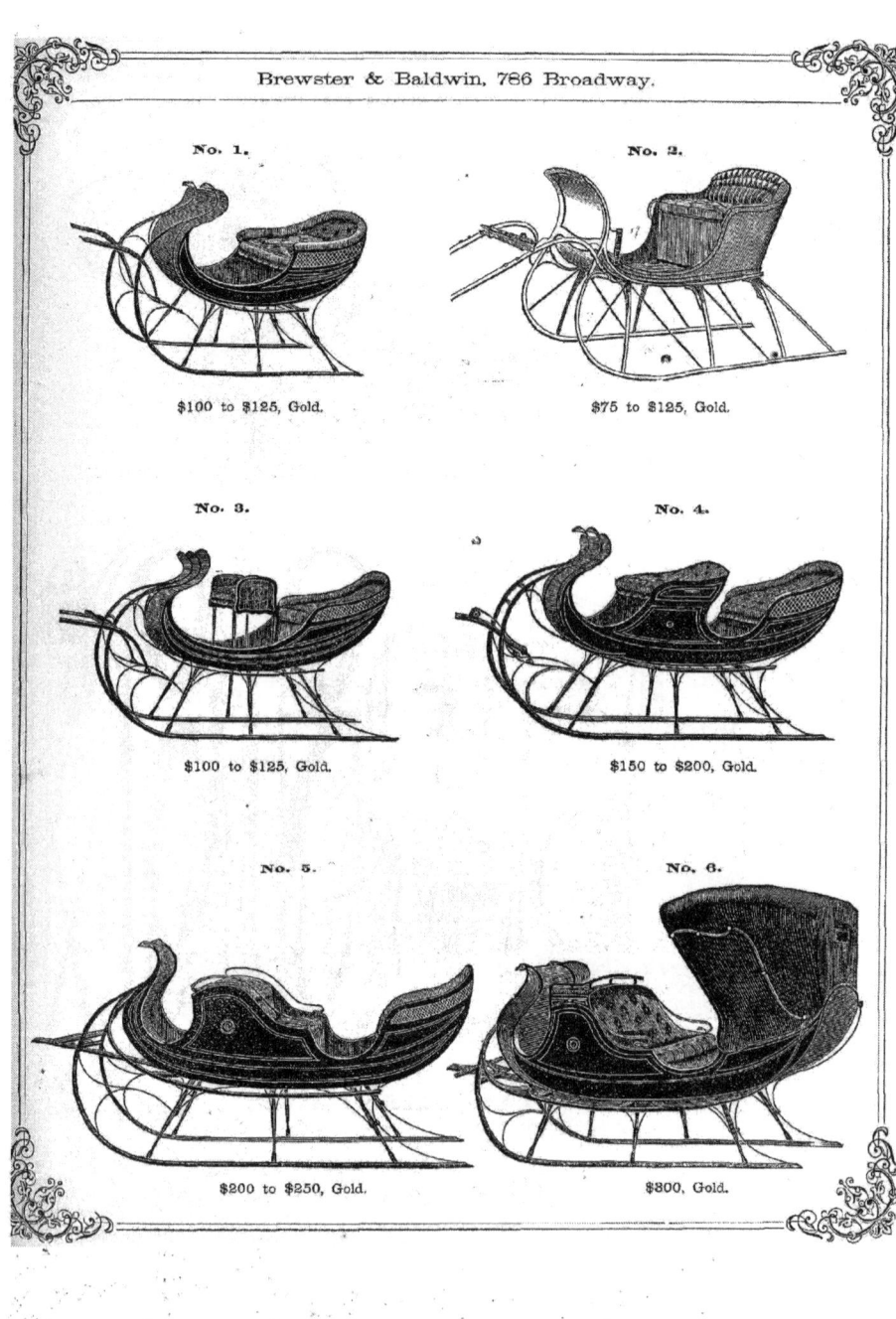

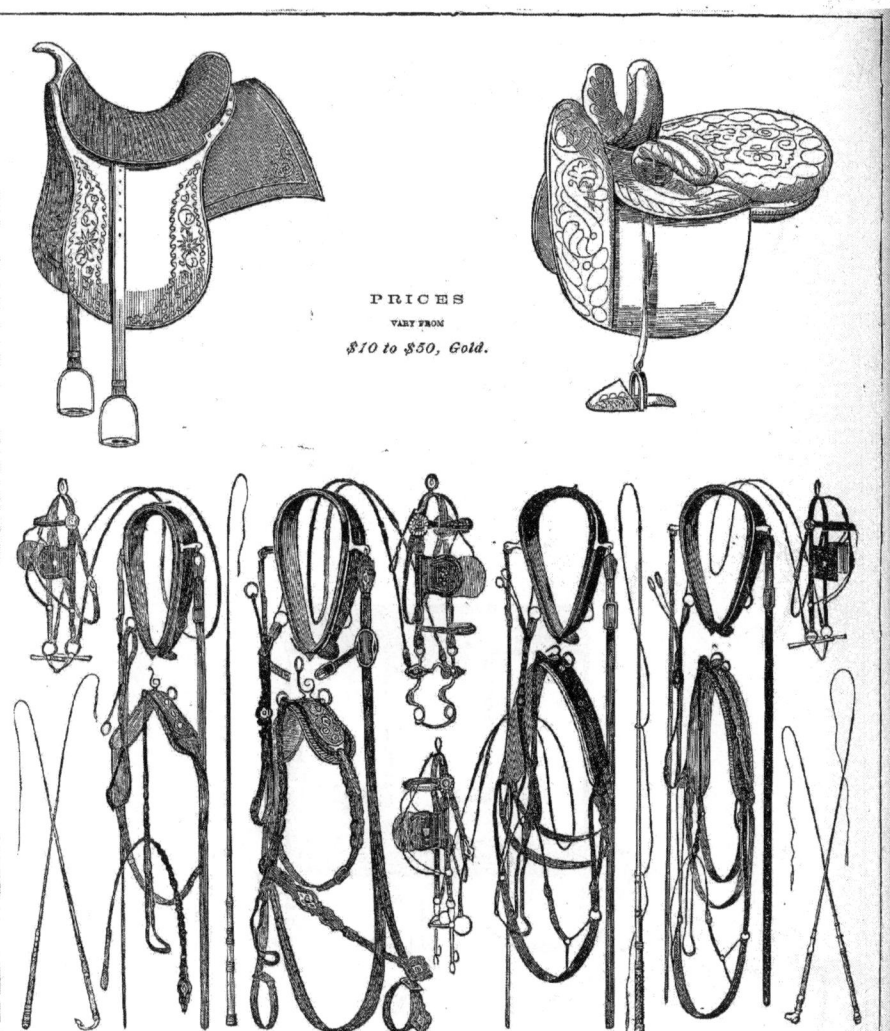

PRICES
VARY FROM
$10 to $50, Gold.

Whips, $3 to $10.
Plain Single Harness, $20 to $30.   Fine Single Harness, $40 to $75.
Light Shifting Harness, $50 to $85.   Coach Harness, $75 to $150.

Brewster & Baldwin, 786 Broadway.

No. 950. $175 to $225, Gold.

Standing top Doctor's Phaeton.
Faeton de Doctor; sombrero alto.

No. 951. $200 to $250, Gold.

Jump-seat Rockaway.
Rockaway con asiento bricando.

Brewster & Baldwin, 786 Broadway.

No. 952. $250 to $300, Gold.

Very nice, stylish jump-seat Rockaway, for one horse.

Rockaway asiento brincando; muy lindo y muy al estilo de un caballo.

No. 953. $250 to $300, Gold.

Same as above—shown with seat jumped forward to carry two.

Mismo que el No. 952 mostrado, con asiento brincado en frente para dos passajeros.

Brewster & Baldwin, 786 Broadway.

No. 954. $250 to $300, Gold.

Jaggar Boat-Wagon, with movable top and movable back seat. Very light, for one horse, and very stylish. Curtains which roll down are of enameled cloth. Pole and shafts. Hung on two Eliptical springs and perch.

Carro Taggar de bote, con sombrero y asiento detras movible, ligero para un caballo y muy al estilo; cortinas doblando son de paño enamelado; lanza y flecha; suportado por dos resortes Eliptico y alcandara.

No. 955. $275 to $325, Gold.

Boat-Wagon, for one and two horses, with movable top and movable back seat. Curtains of the top are of enameled cloth. It is hung on two springs and perch. Pole and shafts.

Carro de bote, de un ó dos caballos; con sombrero y asiento detras movible; cortinas del sombrero son de paño de enamel; suportado por dos resortes y alcandara; con lanza y flecha.

Brewster & Baldwin, 786 Broadway.

No. 956. $300 to $350, Gold.

Very light one-horse Rockaway. Front seat turns over against dash for children. Shafts only. Leather curtains. Hung on two springs and perch.
Rockaway, muy ligero de un caballo; asiento de frente se baja para niños; dos lanzas solamente cortinas de cuero; suportado por dos resortes y alcandara.

No. 957. $300 to $350, Gold.

New style Philadelphia jump-seat Rockaway. Front seat goes forward to the dash for children—the back seat comes up and takes its place. A very light and useful one-horse family carriage. Shafts only. Best leather curtains, and best workmanship. Hung on two Eliptical springs and perch.
Rockaway Filadelphia nuevo estilo, bricando asiento de frente para niños se muda otro de frente tomando su lugar; un carrauje muy ligero y util de un caballo para familia; dos lanzas solamente; cortinas de lo mejor; suportado por resortes Eliptico y alcandara.

Brewster & Baldwin, 786 Broadway.

No. 958. $300 to $375, Gold.

Light one-horse O. G. Rockaway, with leather curtains Shafts only. A very neat and tasteful carriage. Hung on two Eliptical springs and perch.
O. G. Rockaway ligero de un caballo; cortinas de cuero; dos lanzas solamente; un carruaje muy lindo y a gusto; suportado por dos resortes Eliptico y alcandara.

No. 959. $300 to $375, Gold.

Low-door Fenton Rockaway. Imitation cane-work on side. Very light, for one horse. Best leather curtains. Hung on two springs and perch. Shafts only.
Rockaway Fenton puerta baja los lados imitacion de caña; muy ligero para un caballo; cortinas mejores de cuero; suportado por dos resortes y alcandara; dos lanzas solamente.

Brewster & Baldwin, 786 Broadway.

No. 960. $325 to $375, Gold.

Sash-door, one-horse light Rockaway. Hung on two springs and perch. A neat and useful family carriage. Shafts only. Rockaway, puerta de vidriera; ligero para un caballo; suportado por dos resortes y alcandara; un carruaje lindo y util de familia.

No. 961. $325 to $375, Gold.

O. G. back, sash-door, light one-horse four-passenger Rockaway. Hung on two springs and perch.
O. G. Rockaway, detras puerta de vidriera; ligero de un caballo, para cuatro passajeros; suportado por dos resortes y alcandara.

Brewster & Baldwin, 786 Broadway.

No. 962. $340 to $385, Gold.

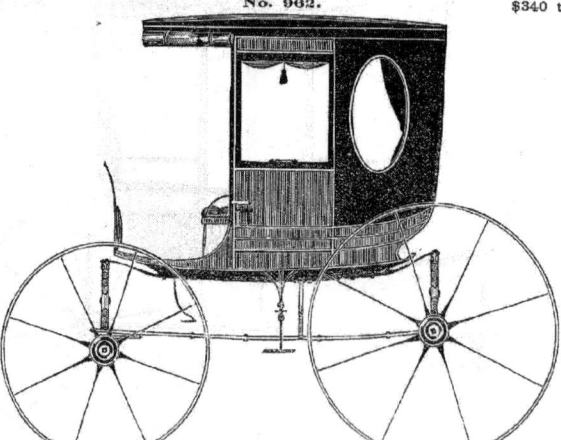

Sash-door, one-horse light four-passenger Rockaway. Oval light in side, and paneled back, with window to drop. Rockaway, ligero de un caballo, para cuatro passajeros; puerta de vidriera; ventana oval a los lados y albardon detras con ventana bajando.

BREWSTER & BALDWIN,
MANUFACTURERS OF
FIRST CLASS CARRIAGES,
786 BROADWAY.

Next to Grace Church.]   Cor. of Tenth Street.
NEW YORK.

ILLUSTRATED CATALOGUES FURNISHED AT REQUEST.

Brewster & Baldwin, 786 Broadway.

No. 963. $350 to $400, Gold.

One-horse Elm City low-door Rockaway, for four persons. Wheels cut under. Belt of French carved wood through the body. Hung on two springs and perch. Pole and shafts.

Rockaway de la ciudad de Elm, de un caballo; cortada para ruedas en frente; cinturon de madera Frances grabado dentro del cuerpo; suportado por dos resortes y alcandara; lanza y flecha.

No. 964. $350 to $400, Gold.

O. G. back, fine four-passenger, low-door, Germantown Rockaway. Hung on two springs and perch. A very commodious carriage for four persons. Pole and shafts. Front wheels cut under for short turn.

Alemania O. G. detras; puerta baja; suportado por dos resortes y alcandara; un curruaje muy conveniente para cuatro personajes; lanza y varas; cortado para ruedas de frente para corta vuelta.

Brewster & Baldwin, 786 Broadway.

No. 965. $375 to $450 Gold.

Four-passenger, sash-door, O. G. back Rockaway. Front wheels cut under for short turn. Belt of carved wood through body. Hung on two springs, with perch. Pole and shafts and lamps.
Rockaway O. G. por detras; puerta de vidriera; para cuatro pasajeros; cortado para ruedas de frente para corta vuelta; cinturon de madera grabado por dentro del cuerpo; suportado por dos resortes y alcandara; lanza varas y lamparas.

No. 966. $375 to $450, Gold.

Four-passenger Charlotte Rockaway. Sash-door. Front wheels to turn under. Hung on two springs and perch. Pole and shafts. A very stylish and light family carriage.
Rockaway Carocin, para cuatro pasajeros; puerta de vidriera; cortado para ruedas de frente; suportado por dos resortes y alcandara; lanza y varas; un carruaje muy ligero y al estilo para familia.

Brewster & Baldwin, 786 Broadway.

No. 967. $500 to $600, Gold.

O. G. back, sash-door, four-passenger Rockaway Coupé. Oval light on sides; back paneled, with glass to drop; division between the driver and those inside movable at pleasure. Pole and shafts. Hung on two springs and perch.

Rockaway Coupe O. G. detras; puerta de vidriera, para cuatro passajeros; ventana oval por los lados; albardon detras, con ventana bajando una division entre el asiento del cochero y los de a dentro movible a voluntad; lanza y varas; suportado por resortes y alcandara.

No. 968. $550 to $650, Gold.

Very stylish Coupé Rockaway, with sash-door; paneled back-quarter. Driving-seat separated by a movable partition, which has two windows in it. Hung on platform springs. Pole and shafts. Imitation blinds in door.

Rockaway Coupé; muy de estilo, puerta de vidriera; albardon detras; una division entre el asiento del cochero y los de a dentro por una particion movible el cual tiene dos ventanas; suportado por resortes de plataforma; lanza y varas; imitacion de blindajes en puerta.

Brewster & Baldwin, 786 Broadway.

No. 969. $550 to $650, Gold.

Very stylish Coupé Rockaway, with sash-door and imitation blinds in it. Oval window in back-quarter. Hung on platform springs. Has division, with windows in it, between the driver and those inside, which is movable at pleasure. Pole and shafts.

Rockaway Coupe muy al estilo, puerta de vidrieras, con imitacion de blindajes; ventana oval en cuartos detras; suportado por resortes de plataforma; una division y ventana; entre el asiento del cochero y los de a dentro movible a voluntad; lanza y varas.

No. 970.

Sash-door, four-passenger Coupé Rockaway. Oval light in sides; paneled back. Movable division between the driver and those inside. Pole and shafts. Hung on two springs.

Rockaway Coupe; puerta de vidriera para cuatro pasajeros; ventana oval a los lados; albardon detras; una division movible entre el asiento del cochero y los de adentro lanza y varas; suportado por dos resortes.

Brewster & Baldwin, 786 Broadway.

No. 967. $500 to $600, Gold.

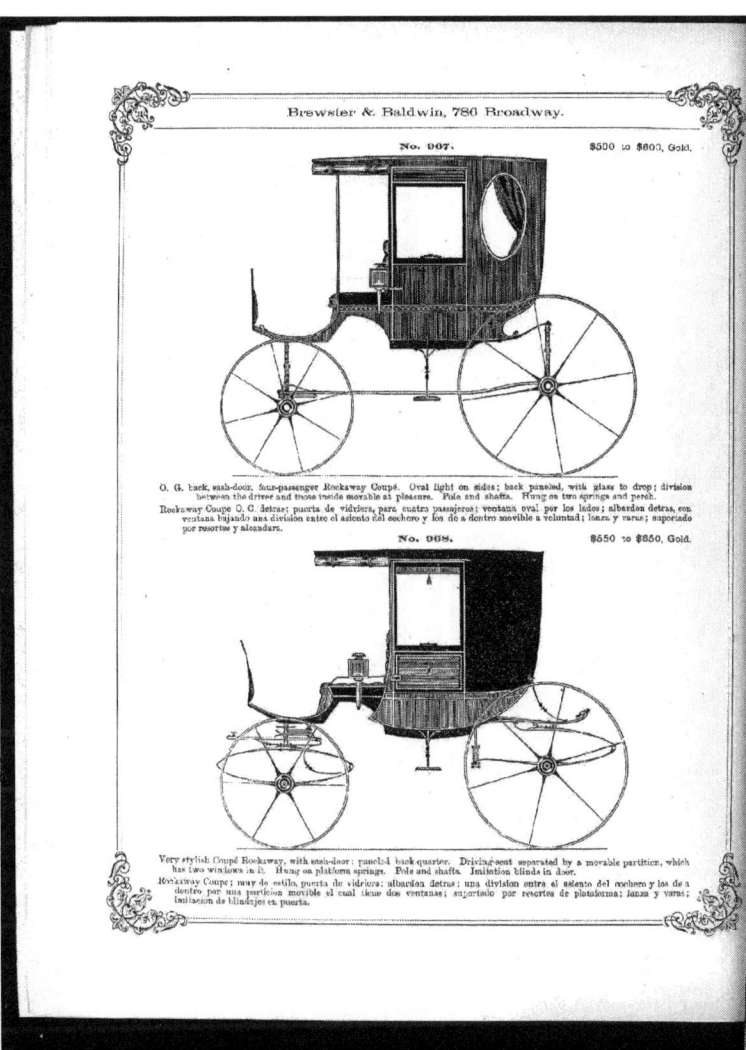

O. G. back, sash-door, four-passenger Rockaway Coupé. Oval light on sides; back paneled, with glass to drop; division between the driver and those inside movable at pleasure. Pole and shafts. Hung on two springs and perch.

Rockaway Coupé O. G. detras; puerta de vidriera, para cuatro pasajeros; ventana oval por los lados; albardon detras, con ventana bajando una division entre el asiento del cochero y los de a dentro movible a voluntad; lanza y varas; soportado por resortes y alsandars.

No. 968. $550 to $650, Gold.

Very stylish Coupé Rockaway, with sash-door; paneled back quarter. Driving-seat separated by a movable partition, which has two windows in it. Hung on platform springs. Pole and shafts. Imitation blinds in door.

Rockaway Coupé; muy de estilo, puerta de vidriera; albardon detras; una division entre el asiento del cochero y los de a dentro por una particion movible el cual tiene dos ventanas; soportado por resortes de plataforma; lanza y varas; imitacion de blindajes en puerta.

Brewster & Baldwin, 786 Broadway.

No. 969. $550 to $650, Gold.

Very stylish Coupé Rockaway, with sash-door and imitation blinds in it. Oval window in back-quarter. Hung on platform springs. Has division, with windows in it, between the driver and those inside, which is movable at pleasure. Pole and shafts.

Rockaway Coupé muy al estilo, puerta de vidrieras, con imitacion de blindajes; ventana oval en cuartos detras; soportado por resortes de plataforma; una division y ventana; entre el asiento del cochero y los de a dentro movible a voluntad; lanza y varas.

No. 970.

Sash-door, four-passenger Coupé Rockaway. Oval light in sides; paneled back. Movable division between the driver and those inside. Pole and shafts. Hung on two springs.

Rockaway Coupé; puerta de vidriera para cuatro pasajeros; ventana oval a los lados; albardon detras; una division movible entre el asiento del cochero y los de adentro lanza y varas; soportado por dos resortes.

Brewster & Baldwin, 786 Broadway.

No. 971. $500 to $600, Gold.

Four-passenger light extension-top Barouche. Top throws down for sun-down use. Hung on four Eliptical springs. Pole and shafts. Front wheels cut under for short turn.
Barouche ligero, sombrero a estencion y bajando cuando no hay sol; suportado por cuatro resortes Eliptico; lanza y varas; cortado para ruedas de frente para corta vuelta.

No. 972. $525 to $625, Gold.

Extension-top "Cabriolet Victoria," for four persons. Fenders over hind wheels. Top all throws back for sun-down use. Hung on platform springs. Pole and shafts.
Victoria Cabriolete; sombrero a estencion, para cuatro passajeros; defensas sobre ruedas detras sombrero bajando cuando no hay sol; lanza y varas; suportado por resortes de plataforma.

Brewster & Baldwin, 786 Broadway.

No. 973. $375 to $425, Gold.

Five-seat extension-top Barouche, for one horse. Top all throws back for sun-down use. Hung on two springs, with perch. A very light and very useful one-horse family carriage.
Barouche; sombrero a estencion, con cinco asientos, de un caballo; sombrero bajando cuando no hay sol; suportado por dos resortes y alcandara; un carruaje muy ligero y util de un caballo, para familia.

No. 974. $750 to $950, Gold.

Extension-top McAllister Brett. A very light and elegant family carriage. Fenders over both front and hind wheels. Hung on platform springs. For one or two horses. Top all throws back for sun-down use.
Brett McAllister; sombrero a estencion, muy ligero y elegante para familia; defensas sobre ruedas de frente y detras; suportado por resortes de plataforma; para un ò dos caballos; sombrero bajando cuando no hay sol.

Brewster & Baldwin, 786 Broadway.

No. 975. $375 to $475, Gold.

One-horse, new-style, four-passenger, light extension-top Barouche, with low doors. Fenders over hind wheels. Hung on two springs and perch. Top all throws back for sun-down use.

Barouche ligero; sombrero a estencion; muy al estilo, de un caballo, para cuatro passajeros con ventanas; defensas sobre ruedas detras; suportado por dos resortes y alcandara; sombrero bajando cuando no hay sol.

No. 976. $375 to $475, Gold

Bowl-pattern, extension-top Barouche, for one or two horses. Hung on two springs and perch. Top all throws back for sun-down use.

Barouche Bowl; sombrero de modo a estencion; de un ò dos caballos; suportado por dos resortes y alcandara; sombrero bajando cuando no hay sol.

Brewster & Baldwin, 786 Broadway.

No. 978. $375 to $475, Gold.

One-horse light extension-top Victoria Cabriolet, with fenders over hind wheels. Hung on two springs and perch. Top all throws back for sun-down use. Pole and shafts. A very elegant carriage for park or country driving.

Victoria Cabrioleto, ligero; sombrero a estencion de un caballo; defensas sobre ruedas detras; suportado por dos resortes y alcandara; sombrero bajándo cuando no hay sol; lanza y varas; un carruaje muy elegante de familia, para el parque ó el campo.

No. 979. $325 to $425, Gold.

One-horse extension-top Barouche; light and very elegant. Hung on two springs and perch. Back-board to carry light trunk or servant. Front wheels cut under for short turn. Top all throws back for sun-down use.

Barouche; sombrero a estencion, de un caballo; ligero y muy elegante; suportado por dos resortes y alcandara; tabla detras para baul ligero ó criado; cortado para ruedas de frente para corta vuelta; sombrero bajando cuando no hay sol.

Brewster & Baldwin, 786 Broadway.

No. 980. $325 to $425 Gold.

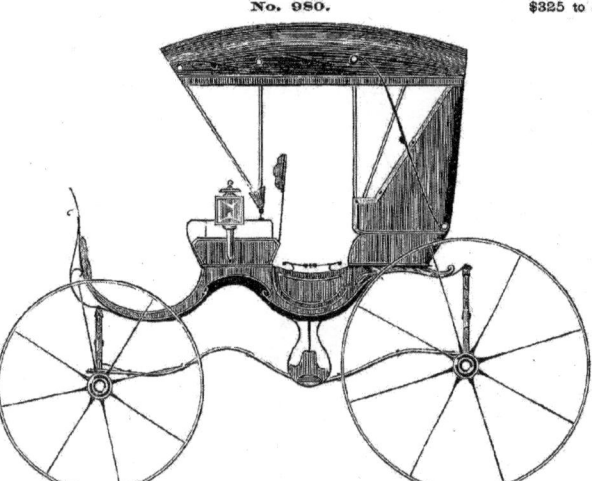

Light one horse, four-passenger, extension-top Barouche. Hung on two springs and perch. Front wheels cut under for short turn. Top all throws back for sun-down use. Pole and shafts and back-board for servant boy or for trunk.

Barouche; sombrero a estencion; de un caballo; ligero; para cuatro passajeros; suportado por dos resortes y alcandara; cortado para ruedas de frente para corta vuelta; sombrero bajando cuando no hay sol; lanza varas y tabla detras para baul ó criado.

No. 990. $225 to $300, Gold.

Six-passenger wagon for country use. Seats all take out and tail-board drops, so that a load of baggage may be carried. Hung on two springs and perch. A strong and very useful carriage.

Carro de Arrendatario, para seis passajeros; asientos se quitan todos y tabla detras baja para poner una cargo por dentro; suportado por dos resortes y alcandara; un carruaje muy fuerte y util.

Brewster & Baldwin, 786 Broadway.

No. 995. $450 to $600, Gold.

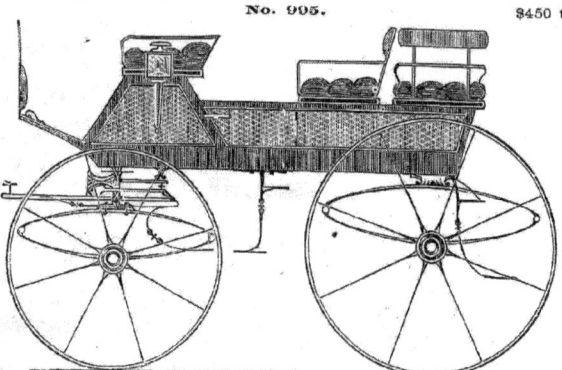

New style American Wagonnette. Hung on four Eliptical springs. Door in the back and at the sides. Carries six passengers in the most compact form. Imitation cane-work on the sides. Driving-seat high enough for driving four horses.

Carreton Americano, nuevo estilo; suportado por cuatro resortes Eliptico; puerta detras y a lados; eleva seis pasajeros en el modo mas solido; los lados con imitacion de caña; asiento del cochero bastante alto para conducir cuatro caballos.

No. 996. $600 to $700, Gold.

"Wagonnette," carrying eight passengers, including driver. Hung on four Eliptical springs. Imitation cane-work on the sides. Front wheels cut under. Entrance in the back. An elegant country carriage.

Carreton, para ocho pasajeros, incluso el cochero; suportado por cuatro resortes Eliptico; los lados con imitacion de caña; cortado para ruedas de frente; entrada detras; un carruaje muy elegante para el campo.

Brewster & Baldwin, 786 Broadway.

No. 1000.

Four-passenger Willow Phaeton. Hung low on four Eliptical springs. Fender over hind wheel; front wheel cut under. Elegant for watering-places. Pole and shafts.

Faeton de Sauce, para cuatro passajeros; pajo y sobre cuatro resortes Eliptico; defensas para ruedas detras; cortado para ruedas de frente; elegante para lugares de paseo; lanza y varas.

No. 1001. $450 to $550, Gold.

Willow "Vis-a-Vis." Dickey seat movable. Front wheels cut under. An elegant watering-place carriage. Pole and shafts.

"Vis-a-Vis" de Sauce; asiento de dickey movible; cortado para ruedas de frente; elegante para lugares de paseo; lanza y varas.

Brewster & Baldwin, 786 Broadway.

No. 1003. $400 to $500, Gold.

Schell pony Phaeton, for ladies' use. Rumble behind for groom. Fenders over front and hind wheels. Hung on platform springs. Usually driven with one horse, or pair small ponies. Willow Phaetons of same shape at $50 less.

Faeton Schill de caballita, para uso de señora; asiento detras para lacayo; defensas sobre ambas ruedas; suportado por resortes de plataforma; generalmente arreglado para un caballo ó dos caballitos; Faetons de Sauce del mismo modo a 50 pesos menos.

No. 1004. $350 to $450, Gold.

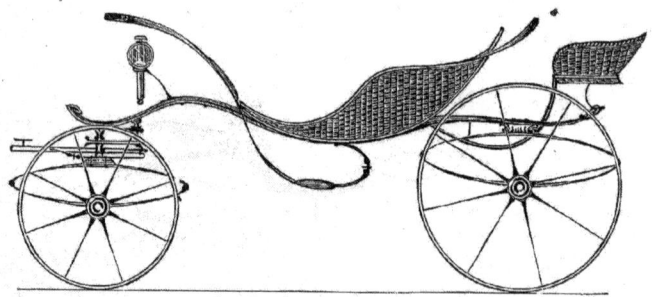

The Willow Phaeton, for ladies' use. Fenders over both wheels. Willow-rumble for groom. Front wheels cut under. Hung on four Eliptical springs. Very light; used with either one horse or pair small ponies. Much in use at the watering-places.

Faeton de Sauce, para uso de señora; defensas sobre ambas ruedas asiento de Sauce para lacayo; cortado para ruedas de frente; suportado por cuatro resortes Eliptico; muy ligero, usado con un caballo ó dos caballitos; muy usado en lugares de paseo.

Brewster & Baldwin, 786 Broadway.

No. 1005. $400 to $500, Gold.

Very low-swung "Willow Phaeton," for ladies' use. Fenders over front and hind wheels. Very closely coupled. Light rumble for servant. Drawn with one horse or pair of ponies. Hung on four Elliptical springs.

Faeton de Sauce de Balancin, para uso de señora; muy bajo; defensas sobre ambas ruedas; muy estrechamente juntado; asiento ligero para lacayo; usado con un caballo ó dos caballitos; suportado por cuatro resortes Elíptico.

No. 1006. $300 to $350, Gold.

Willow Phaeton. Hung on three springs and perch. Fender over hind wheels. Very light and very stylish. Shafts only.

Faeton; suportado por tres resortes y alcandara; defensas sobre ruedas detras; muy ligero y muy al estilo; varas solamente.

Brewster & Baldwin, 786 Broadway.

No. 1010. $400 to $450, Gold.

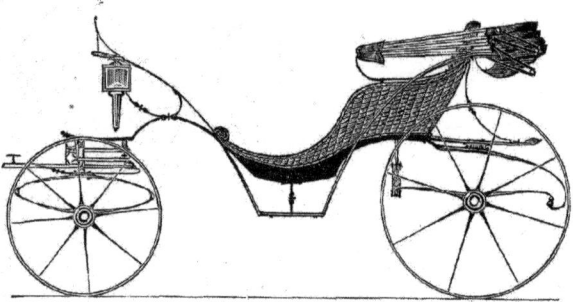

Willow Phaeton, with top. Hung on platform springs. Front wheels cut under. Hangs quite low, and easy of access. Top takes off at pleasure. Pole and shafts.

Faeton de Sauce con sombrero; suportado por resortes de plataforma; cortado para ruedas de frente; muy bajo y facil de acceso; sombrero se quita a voluntad; lanza y varas.

No. 1011. $425 to $475, Gold.

Same as above, except the servant's seat.

Mismo que el No. 1,010, a escepcion que tiene asiento para lacayo.

Brewster & Baldwin, 786 Broadway.

No. 1015. $325 to $375, Gold.

George IV Pony Phaeton. Imitation cane sides. Front wheels cut under for short turn. Hung on two springs and perch. Very neat and pretty one-horse trap. Shafts only; pole could be fitted.

Faeton "George 4to," de dos caballitos; lados con imitacion de caña; cortado para ruedas de frente para corta vuelta; suportado por resortes y alcandara; un carruaje muy lindo y bonito de un caballo; varas solamente; lanza se puede ajustar.

No. 1016. $350 to $400, Gold.

George IV Pony Phaeton, with rumble for servant. Hung on three Eliptical springs. Front wheel cut under for short turn. Very neat and pretty one-horse trap. Shafts only; pole could be fitted.

Faeton George 4to de caballito; asiento para lacayo; suportado por tres resortes Eliptico; cortado para ruedas de frente; un carruaje muy lindo y bonito de un caballo; varas solamente; lanza se puede ajustar.

Brewster & Baldwin, 786 Broadway.

No. 1020. $275 to $325, Gold.

Light Willow Buggy, for one horse or pair of ponies. Front wheels cut under for short turn. Hung on two springs and perch. A very light and very elegant wagon for ladies' use. Shafts only; pole could be fitted.

Coche Buggy de Sauce ligero; de un caballo ó dos caballitos; cortado para ruedas de frente para corta vuelta; suportado por dos resortes y alcandara; un carruaje muy ligero y muy elegante para el uso de señora; varas solamente; lanza se puede ajustar.

No. 1021. $325 to $375, Gold.

New-style four-spring, no-top, Park Wagon. Very comfortable. Front wheels cut under; seat painted imitation cane. Shafts only; pole could be added.

Carro de Parque, nuevo estilo; cuatro resortes y no sombrero; muy agradable; cortado para ruedas de frente; asiento juntado imitacion de caña; varas solamente; lanza se puede ajustar.

Brewster & Baldwin, 786 Broadway.

No. 1022. $250 to $300, Gold.

Baldwin Pony Wagon. Carries two ladies and two children; children enter behind, preventing the possibility of being run over; also, making the wagon very compact. Hung on two springs and perch. Front wheels cut under for short turn. Shafts only; pole could be fitted.

Carro Baldwin de caballito; para dos señoras y dos niños; entrada para niños detras una prevencion de peligro; asi mismo haciendolo muy solido; suportado por dos resortes y alcandara; cortado para ruedas de frente para corta vuelta; varas solamente; lanza se puede ajustar.

No. 1023. $325 to $375, Gold.

"Pony Wagonnette." Carries four passengers; two enter at the rear, and sit vis-a-vis. Front wheels cut under. Hung on four Eliptical springs. Pole and shafts. One of the most unique Pony Phaetons we build.

Carreton de Caballitos, para cuatro passajeros; entruda detras y asiento frente a frente; cortado para ruedas de frente; suportado por cuatro resortes Eliptico; lanza y varas; un de los unicos Faetons de caballitos que hacemos.

Brewster & Baldwin, 786 Broadway.

No. 1027. $400 to $500, Gold.

Square-box, four-passenger, light one-horse Wagon. Top shifts and seats shift. Can be made into a buggy. Hung on two Eliptical springs. Pole and shafts.

Carro cuadrado, para cuatro passajeros; ligero de un caballo; sombrero y asiento cambian detras de frente; puede hacerse de Buggy; suportado por dos resortes Eliptico; lanza y varas.

BREWSTER & BALDWIN,
MANUFACTURERS OF
FIRST CLASS CARRIAGES,
786 BROADWAY,
Next to Grace Church.]   Cor. of Tenth Street.
NEW YORK.

ILLUSTRATED CATALOGUES FURNISHED AT REQUEST.

Brewster & Baldwin, 786 Broadway.

No. 1028. $300 to $400, Gold.

Shifting slide-seat Top-Wagon, for two or four persons at pleasure. (See plate below, No. 1,029.) Pole and shafts. Hung on two Eliptical springs and perch. A very light and very useful family Buggy.

Carro, con sombrero y asiento mudando; para dos ó cuatro passajeros a voluntad; ve el plan No. 1,029; lanza y varas; suportado por dos resortes Eliptico y alcandara; un Buggy muy ligero y muy util de familia.

No. 1029. $300 to $400, Gold.

Same as No. 1,028; shown for two persons.

Mismo que el No. 1,028; mostrada para dos personages.

Brewster & Baldwin, 786 Broadway.

No. 1030. $350 to $425, Gold.

New style slide-seat Top-Buggy, for two or four at pleasure. (See plate below, No. 1,013.) One or two horses. A neat and useful family wagon.
Coche Buggy nuevo estilo, con asiento y sombrero mudando; para dos ó cuatro passajeros a voluntad; ve el plan No. 1,031; de un ó dos caballos; un carro lindo y util de familia.

No. 1031. $350 to $425, Gold.

Same as above.
Mismo que el No. 1,030, para dos.

Brewster & Baldwin, 786 Broadway.

No. 1032. $375 to $450, Gold.

Slide-seat Top Wagon; also, extension-top combined, as shown in plate below. For one or two horses. A light and useful family Buggy.

Carro; con asiento y sombrero mudando; sombrero a estencion; combinado como mostrado in el No. 1,033; de un ó dos caballos; un Buggy ligero y util de familia.

No. 1033. $375 to $450, Gold.

Same as above, shown as extension-top.
Mismo que el No. 1,032; con sombrero a estencion.

Brewster & Baldwin, 786 Broadway.

No. 1034. $300 to $350, Gold.

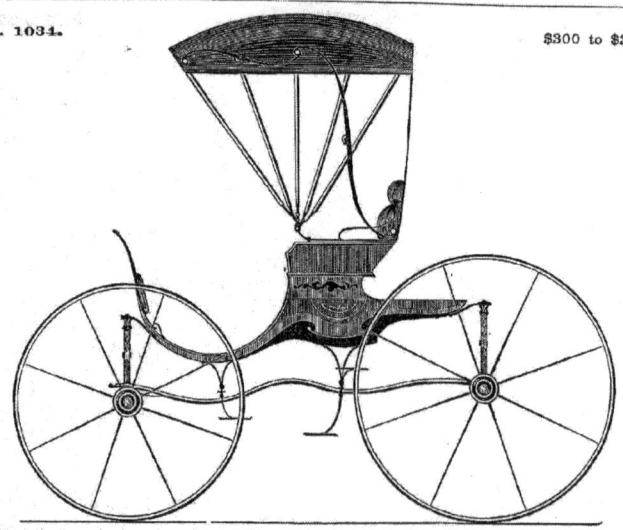

Slide-seat Buggy, for two or four persons at pleasure. (See cut below, No. 1,035.) Hung on two springs and perch. Pole and shafts.
Coche Buggy; asiento mudando; para dos ó cuatro passajeros a voluntad; ve el plan No. 1,035; suportado por dos resortes y alcandara; lanza y varas.

No. 1035. $300 to $350, Gold.

Same as above, shown for four persons.
Mismo que el No. 1,034; mostrado para cuatro passajeros.

Brewster & Baldwin, 786 Broadway.

No. 1036. $335 to $400, Gold.

Slide-seat, extension-top Buggy. Carries four, if desirable. (See plate below, No. 1,037.) Pole and shafts. Hung on two Eliptical springs.
Coche Buggy, con asiento y mudando, sombrero a estencion; para cuatro passajeros a voluntad; ve el plan No. 1,037; lanza y varas; suportado por dos resortes Eliptico.

No. 1037. $335 to $400, Gold.

Same as above, shown for four persons.
Mismo que el No. 1,036; mostrado para cuatro passajeros.

Brewster & Baldwin, 786 Broadway.

No. 1038. $300 to $325, Gold.

Slide-seat Buggy; carries two or four at pleasure. One or two horses. Hung on two springs and perch.
Coche Buggy; asiento mudando; lleva dos ó cuatro a voluntad; de un ó dos caballos; suportado por dos resortes y alcandara.

No. 1039. $275 to $325, Gold.

Cut-under top-Buggy; shifting side-curtains; back seat folds out for groom or children. Hung on two springs and porch.
A very useful carriage.
Coche Buggy; cortado para ruedas de frente; cortinas mudando; asiento doblando por detras para lacayo ó niño; suportado por dos resortes y alcandara; un carruaje muy util.

Brewster & Baldwin, 786 Broadway.

No. 1040. $275 to $325, Gold.

Coal-box top-Buggy; back seat folds in. Hung on two springs and perch. Top takes off. Shafts only.
Coche Buggy; pescante y sombrero acarbonado; asiento detras doblando; suportado por dos resortes y alcandara; sombrero se quita; varas solamente.

No. 1041. $275 to $325, Gold.

Top-Buggy, with front wheels cut under for short turn; back seat folds in. Hung on two springs and perch. Shafts only.
Coche Buggy, con sombrero; cortado para ruedas de frente para corta vuelta; asiento detras doblando; suportado por dos resortes y alcandara; varas solamente.

Brewster & Baldwin, 786 Broadway.

No. 1043. $400 to $450, Gold.

Elegant four-spring shifting-top Buggy; front wheels cut under. Hangs high. Pole and shafts.

Coche Buggy, sombrero mudando, elegante; sobre cuatro resortes; cortado para ruedas de frente, alto; lanza y varas.

No. 1044. $350 to $400, Gold.

Boston cut-under, with box behind for sundries. Hung on two springs and perch. Shafts only.

Coche Buggy de Boston: cortado para ruedas de frente; con caja detras por mercancias; suportado por dos resortes y alcandara; varas solamente.

Brewster & Baldwin, 786 Broadway.

No. 1045. $175 to $225, Gold.

Light Southern Buggy, with front wheels to cut under for short turn. Baggage-rack or seat for servant. Hung on two springs and perch. Top shifts. Shafts only.

Coche Buggy del Sur; cortado para ruedas de frente para corta vuelta; tabla para baul ó lacayo; suportado por dos resortes y alcandara; sombrero mudando; varas solamente.

No. 1046. $175 to $225, Gold.

Cut-under, shifting-top Buggy; front wheels cut under for short turn. Hung on two springs and perch. Shafts only.

Coche Buggy; cortado para ruedas de frente y sombrero mudando; cortado para corta vuelta; suportado por dos resortes y alcandara; varas solamente.

Brewster & Baldwin, 786 Broadway.

No. 1047. $175 to $225, Gold.

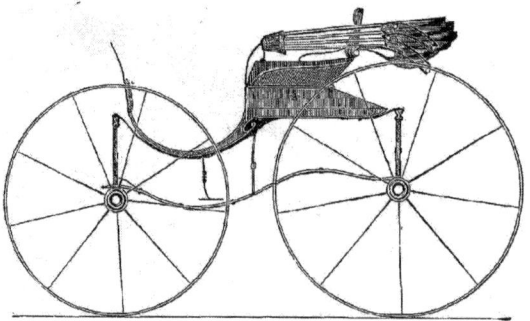

Southern shifting-top Buggy. Hangs low, and easy of access, on two springs and perch. Shafts only.

Buggy del Sur; sombrero mudando; suportado por dos resortes y alcandara; bajo y facil de acceso; varas solamente.

No. 1048. $175 to $225, Gold.

Southern-style light shifting-top Buggy. Hangs low, and easy of access, on two springs and perch. Shafts only.

Buggy del Sur; ligero y al estilo; sombrero mudando; bajo y facil de acceso; suportado por dos resortes y alcandara; varas solamente.

Brewster & Baldwin, 786 Broadway.

No. 1049. $175 to $225, Gold.

Duplicate of No. 1,048, except that it has a paneled seat.

Mismo que el No. 1,048, a escepcion que tiene un asiento de albardon.

No. 1050. $300 to $350, Gold.

Yacht Buggy. Very light and elegant road-wagon, with shifting-top and shifting side-curtains. Hung on two springs, with perch. Shafts only. The very finest work made.

Buggy Yate; un carro muy ligero y elegante para el camino; sombrero y cortinas mudando; suportado por dos resortes y alcandara; varas solamente el mas hermoso.

Brewster & Baldwin, 786 Broadway.

No. 1051. $250 to $300, Gold.

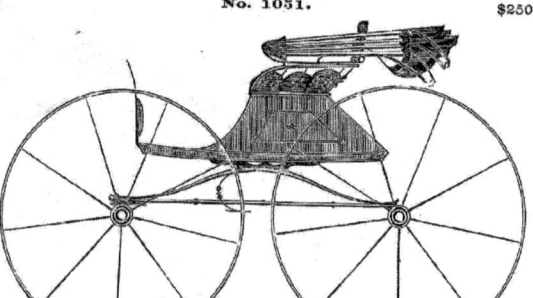

Concord-spring shifting-top York Buggy; shifting side-curtains. Hung on two springs and perch. A very substantial wagon for the country. Shafts only.

Buggy York resortes Concordia; sombrero mudando; cortinas a los lados mudando; suportado por dos resortes y alcandara; un carro muy necessario en el campo; varas solamente.

No. 1052. $300 to $350, Gold.

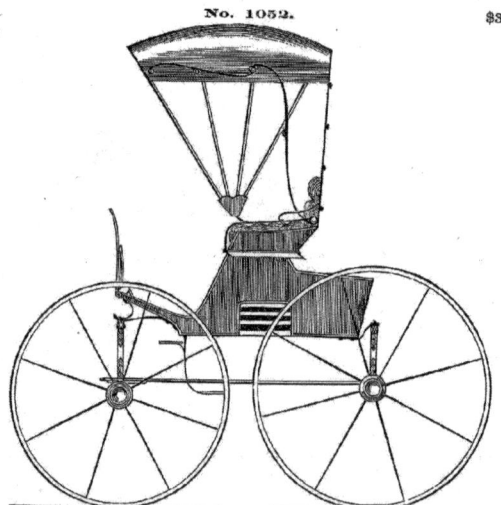

Griswold Buggy, with cleft in side; shifting top. Hung on two springs and perch. An elegant Park wagon. Shafts only. Pole could be added.

Buggy Griswold, con incision en los lados; sombrero mudando; suportado por dos resortes y alcandara; un carro elegante para el parque; varas solamente; lanza se puede ajustar.

Brewster & Baldwin, 786 Broadway.

No. 1053. $300 to $350, Gold.

Surprise Buggy, with *close top*; may shift if preferred. The mouldings on body afford an opportunity for effect in painting. Hung on two springs and perch. Shafts only.

Buggy de Sorpresa; sombrero cerrado puede mundarse si es preferable; el molde da opportunidad a la pintura de hacer effecto; suportado por dos resortes y alcandara; varas solamente.

No. 1054. $300 to $350, Gold.

Coal-box shifting-top Buggy; cane sides; shifting side-curtains. An elegant Park wagon. Hung on two springs and perch. Shafts only.

Buggy pescanto y sombrero acarbonado y mudando; lados de caña; cortinas mudando; un carro elegante para el parque; suportado por dos resortes y alcandara; varas solamente.

Brewster & Baldwin, 786 Broadway.

No. 1055. $300 to $350, Gold.

Bowl Buggy. Light, stylish, and new pattern; shifting top. Hung on two springs and perch. Side-curtains to use at pleasure.

Buggy Bowl ligero, al estilo y nuevo modo; sombrero mudando; suportado por dos resortes y alcandara; cortinas de los lados usados a voluntad.

No. 1056. $300 to $350, Gold.

York Buggy. Very light and very elegant. Paneled over behind; shifting top; shifting side-curtains.

Buggy York; muy ligero y muy elegante; albardon arriba por detras; lados y sombrero mudando.

Brewster & Baldwin, 786 Broadway.

No. 1057. $300 to $350, Gold.

Box Buggy, with low sides; paneled over behind; shifting top; shifting side-curtains. Hung on two springs and perch. A light and stylish wagon. Shafts only.

Buggy pescante; con lados bajos; albardon arriba por detras; sombrero y cortinas mudando; suportado por dos resortes y alcandara; un carro ligero y al estilo; varas solamente.

No. 1058. $175 to $225, Gold.

Box Buggy. Low sides; boot of leather; shifting-top and side-curtains. Hung on two springs and perch. Shafts only.

Buggy pescante; lados bajos; pesebre de cuero; cortinas y sombrero mudando; suportado por dos resortes y alcandara; varas solamente.

Brewster & Baldwin, 786 Broadway.

No. 1059. $300 to $350, Gold.

New style ribbed-side, shifting-top Buggy. A wide and comfortable wagon, with plenty of leg room; stout. Hung on two springs and perch.

Buggy nuevo estilo de costados; sombrero mudando; un carro ancho y agradable con mucho lugar para las piernas fuerte; suportado por dos resortes y alcandara.

No. 1060. $175 to $225, Gold.

Low-side, square-box Buggy. Shifting-top and side-curtains; leather boot. Hung on two springs and perch. Shafts only.

Buggy, pescante cuadrado; lados bajo; cortinas y sombrero mudando; pesebre de cuero; suportado por dos resortes y alcandara; varas solamente.

33

Brewster & Baldwin, 786 Broadway.

No. 1061. $300 to $350, Gold.

Express Wagon. Light and elegant, with ribbed sides, shifting-top and shifting side-curtains. Hung on two springs and perch. Shafts only.

Carro de Correo; ligero y elegante, con costados; sombrero y cortinas a los lados mudando; suportado por dos resortes y alcandara; varas solamente.

No. 1062. $300 to $350, Gold.

Deep-side, square-box, close-top Buggy. Hung on two springs and perch.

Buggy, pescante cuadrado; oscuro lados; sombrero cerrado; suportado por dos resortes y alcandara.

Brewster & Baldwin, 786 Broadway.

No. 1063. $300 to $350, Gold.

Queen's Buggy, with top and shifting side-curtains. Hung low, and much driven by ladies; has two Eliptical springs and perch. Shafts only.

Buggy "Reina," con sombrero y cortinas mudando; bajo y conducido por señoras; suportado por dos resortes Eliptico y alcandara; varas solamente.

No. 1064. $325 to $375, Gold.

Park Phaeton. Hung low; light and stylish; close sides. Hung on two springs and perch. Shafts only.

Phaeton de Parque, bajo; ligero y al estilo; lados cerrado; suportado por dos resortes y alcandara; varas solamente.

Brewster & Baldwin, 786 Broadway.

No. 1065. $175 to $225, Gold.

Southern style light top-Buggy. Shafts only.
Buggy del Sur, al estilo; sombrero cerrado; varas solamente.

No. 1066. $225 to $300, Gold.

Brainard Gig-Phaeton. Low and easy of access. Shifting side-curtains. Hung on two springs and perch.
Buggy "Gig de Brainard;" bajo y facil de acceso; cortinas de los lados mudando; suportado por dos resortes y alcandara.

Brewster & Baldwin, 786 Broadway.

No. 1067. $300 to $350, Gold.

Queen's Buggy, with close sides. Hung low; much driven by ladies. Hung on two Eliptical springs and perch. Shafts only.
Buggy "Reina;" lados cerrado, bajo; conducido por señoras; suportado por dos resortes Eliptico y alcandara; varas solamente.

No. 1068. $275 to $325, Gold.

Gig Phaeton, for Doctor's use. Hung on two Eliptical springs. Shafts only.
Faeton "Gig," para Doctor; suportado por dos resortes Eliptico; varas solamente.

Brewster & Baldwin, 786 Broadway.

No. 1069. $200 to $250, Gold.

Gig Phaeton. Light; for Doctors' use in the country. Hung on two Eliptical springs. Shafts only.

Faeton "Gig," ligero para Doctor del campo; suportado por dos resortes Eliptico; varas solamente.

No. 1080. $140 to $180, Gold.

Southern-style, light, no-top Buggy, with servant's seat, which folds in. Hung on two springs and perch. Shafts only.

Buggy del Sur; ligero de estilo, sin sombrero, con asiento para lacayo doblando por dentro; suportado por dos resortes y alcandara; varas solamente.

Brewster & Baldwin, 786 Broadway.

No. 1081. $200 to $225, Gold.

Light, coal-box, no-top, turn-out-seat Buggy. A light and stylish wagon for Park use. Hung on two springs and perch. Shafts only.

Buggy, ligero; pescante acarbonado; sin sombrero; asiento de vuelta; un carro ligero y al estilo para el uso del parque; suportado por dos resortes y alcandara; varas solamente.

No. 1082. $225 to $275, Gold.

No-top Buggy, with groom's seat, which folds in. Front wheels cut under for short turn. Hung on two springs and perch. Shafts only.

Buggy, sin sombrero; con asiento de lacayo; doblando por dentro; cortado para ruedas de frente para corta vuelta; suportado por dos resortes y alcandara; varas solamente.

Brewster & Baldwin, 786 Broadway.

No. 1083. $225 to $275, Gold.

New-style, coal-box, no-top Buggy, with Stanhope pillar. Back seat folds in. Hung on two springs and perch. Shafts only.

Buggy nuevo estilo, de pescante acarbonado; sin sombrero; coluna de Stanhope; asiento detras doblando por dentro; suportado por dos resortes y alcandara; varas solamente.

BREWSTER & BALDWIN,
MANUFACTURERS OF
FIRST CLASS CARRIAGES,
786 BROADWAY,
Next to Grace Church.]   Cor. of Tenth Street.
NEW YORK.

ILLUSTRATED CATALOGUES FURNISHED AT REQUEST.

Brewster & Baldwin, 786 Broadway.

No. 1084. $200 to $225, Gold.

No-top, jump-seat Box-wagon. Seat behind for boy. Hung on two Eliptical springs, with perch. Shafts only.

Carro, con asiento bricando; sin sombrero; asiento detras de lacayo; suportado por dos resortes Eliptico y alcandara; varas solamente.

No. 1085. $200 to $225, Gold.

Same as above, shown to carry four.

Mismo que el No. 1,084, mostrado para cuatro.

Brewster & Baldwin, 786 Broadway.

No. 1086. $200 to $225, Gold.

Stylish square-box, jump-seat wagon. Hung on two Eliptical springs and perch. Shown with top in No. 1,028. Pole and shafts.

Carro, pescante cuadrado; asiento bricando de estilo; suportado por dos resortes Eliptico y alcandara; mostrado con sombrero en el No. 1,028; lanza y varas.

No. 1087. $200 to $225, Gold.

Same as above, shown to carry two. Same style with top shown in No. 1,029.

Mismo que el No. 1,086, mostrado para dos; mismo estilo de sombrero mostrado en el No. 1,029.

Brewster & Baldwin, 786 Broadway.

No. 1088. $185 to $235, Gold.

No-top, slide-seat Buggy, for two or four persons. (See No. 1,089.) Hung on two springs.

Buggy sin sombrero; asiento mudando, para dos ó cuatro; suportado por dos resortes.

No. 1089. $185 to $235, Gold.

Same as above, shown for two passengers.

Mismo que el No. 1,088, mostrado por dos passajeros.

Brewster & Baldwin, 786 Broadway.

No. 1090. $135 to $165, Gold.

Light Buggy, with lazy back; box behind. Front wheels cut under for short turn. Hung on two springs and perch. Shafts only.

Buggy ligero, con asiento a gusto; caja detras; cortada para ruedas de frente para corta vuelta; suportado por dos resortes y alcandara; varas solamente.

No. 1091. $135 to $165, Gold.

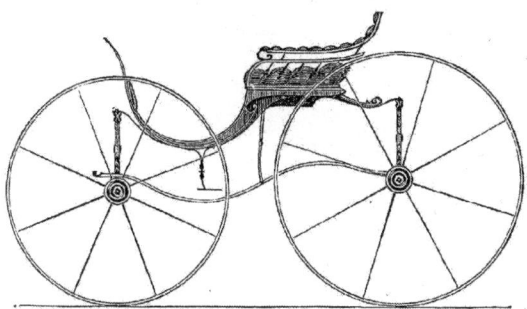

Light Southern Buggy; easy of access. Hung on two springs and perch. Shafts only.

Buggy del Sur; ligero, facil de acceso; suportado por dos resortes y alcandara; varas solamente.

Brewster & Baldwin, 786 Broadway.

No. 1092. $100 to $125, Gold.

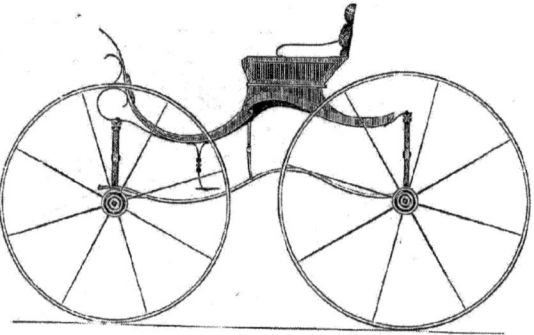

Light, Southern-style, no-top Buggy, with lazy back. Hung on two springs and perch. Shafts only.

Buggy del Sur; de estilo y ligero; con asiento a gusto; suportado por dos resortes y alcandara; varas solamente.

No. 1093. $110 to $135, Gold.

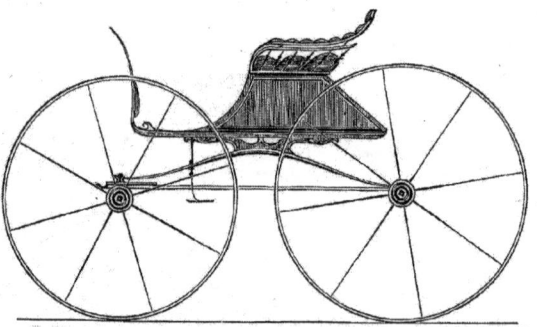

No-top, Concord-spring Buggy. Light and strong. Shafts only.

Buggy resortes de Concordia; sin sombrero; ligero y fuerte; varas solamente.

Brewster & Baldwin, 786 Broadway.

No. 1094. $225 to $300, Gold.

"Woburn-spring," single-seat Trotting-Wagon. This style, for a single seat, gives more strength, with less weight, than any other wagon. Shafts only.

Carro Woburn de trote de un asiento, con resortes; un asiento da mas fuerza y menos peso que cualquiera otro carro; varas solamente.

No. 1095. $225 to $300, Gold.

Side-bar, coal-box Trotting-Wagon. Very light and very stylish. Shafts only.

Carro al trote; bara al lado; pescante acarbonado; muy ligero y muy al estilo; varas solamente.

Brewster & Baldwin, 786 Broadway.

No. 1096. $225 to $300, Gold.

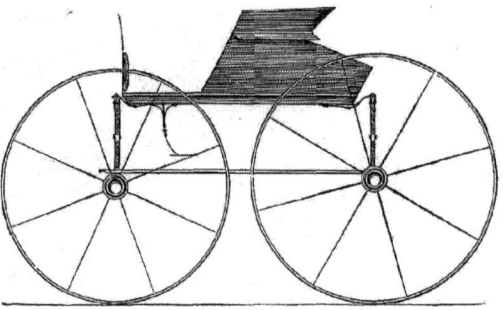

York style, no-top Trotting-Wagon. Hung on two Eliptical springs. Light and very stylish. Shafts only.

Carro de trote estilo de York; suportado por dos resortes Eliptico; ligero y muy al estilo; varas solamente.

No. 1097. $110 to $135, Gold.

Light, no-top Wagon. Leather boot. Hung on two Eliptical springs and perch. Shafts only.

Carro ligero, sin sombrero; pesebre de cuero; suportado por dos Eliptico y alcandara; varas solamente.

Brewster & Baldwin, 786 Broadway.

No. 1098. $200 to $275, Gold.

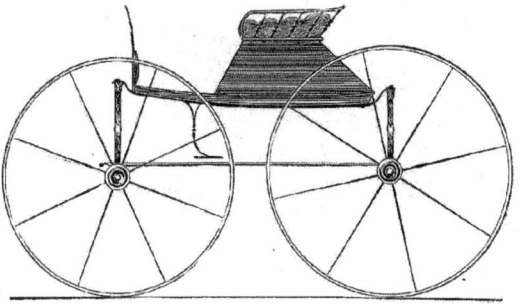

Philadelphia-style, light, no-top Eliptical-spring Buggy, with spindle seat. Shafts only. A very stylish road-wagon.

Buggy estilo de Filadelfia; ligero, sin sombrero; resortes Eliptico; con asiento; varas solamente; un carro de camino muy al estilo.

No. 1099. $110 to $135, Gold.

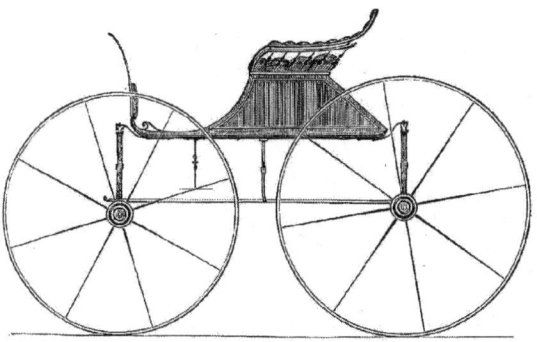

No-top Wagon. Eliptical springs and perch. A neat, plain wagon.

Carro, sin sombrero; resortes Eliptico y alcandara; un lindo y sencillo carro.

Brewster & Baldwin, 786 Broadway.

No. 1100. $225 to $275, Gold.

Surprise Buggy. Hung on two Eliptical springs and perch. Shafts only. Moldings on body afford an opportunity for effect in painting.

Buggy de Sorpresa; suportado por dos resortes Eliptico y alcandara; varas solamente; el molde das opportunidad a la pintura de hacer efficto.

No. 1101. $225 to $275, Gold.

Light Road-Wagon, with Stanhope pillar. An elegant wagon. Hung on two springs and perch. Sits high. Shafts only.

Carro de camino, ligero; coluna de Stanhope; un carro elegante; suportado por dos resortes y alcandara; muy alto; varas solamente.

Brewster & Baldwin, 786 Broadway.

No. 1102. $225 to $275, Gold.

Road-Wagon, with Stanhope pillar and panel in corner of seat. Hung on two springs and perch. Shafts only.

Carro de camino; coluna de Stanhope y albardon en rincon de asiento; suportado por dos resortes y alcaudara; varas solamente.

No. 1103. $225 to $275, Gold.

Coal-box, no-top, light Road-Wagon. Hung on two springs and perch. Shafts only.

Carro de camino; pescante acarbonado; sin sombrero; suportado por dos resortes y alcaudara; varas solamente.

Brewster & Baldwin, 786 Broadway.

No. 1104. $300, Gold.

Road-Wagon, made of willow; usually painted a light color. Makes a stylish and attractive wagon for one horse. Shafts only. Hung on two Eliptical springs and perch.

Carro de camino hecho de sauce; comunmente pintado de color ligero; un carro muy al estilo y de attraccion; de un caballo; varas solamente.

No. 1105. $225 to $275, Gold.

Bowl Buggy. No top. Imitation cane seats. Hung on two springs and perch. Shafts only. A very neat and attractive wagon.

Buggy Bowl; sin sombrero; asientos imitacion de caña; suportado por dos resortes y alcandara; varas solamente; un carro muy lindo y de attraccion.

Brewster & Baldwin, 786 Broadway.

No. 1106. $225 to $275, Gold.

Square-box, no-top Eliptical-spring Wagon. A very favorite style. Shafts only. Pole may be added.

Carro de pescante cuadrado; sin sombrero; resortes Eliptico y un estilo muy favorito; varas solamente; lanza se puede ajustar.

BREWSTER & BALDWIN,
MANUFACTURERS OF
FIRST CLASS CARRIAGES,
786 BROADWAY,
Next to Grace Church.]   Cor. of Tenth Street.
NEW YORK.

ILLUSTRATED CATALOGUES FURNISHED AT REQUEST.

Brewster & Baldwin, 786 Broadway.

No. 1107. $140 to $175, Gold.

Jaggar Wagon. A very useful wagon for the country. Hung on two Eliptical springs. Shafts only. Spindle seat.

Carro Jaggar; un carro de mucho utilidad para el campo; suportado por dos resortes; varas solamente; asiento esplendido.

No. 1110. $200 to $250, Gold.

Four-passenger, no-top Jaggar Wagon. Both seats take out; tail-board drops. A very desirable wagon for depot use. Pole and shafts.

Carro Juggar; sin sombrero; para cuatro passajeros; asientos se quitar; tabla bajo; un carro muy a gusto para un deposito; lanza y varas.

Brewster & Baldwin, 786 Broadway.

No. 1112. $250 to $275, Gold.

Stylish square-box, no-top Wagon, with movable back seat. Hung on two Elliptical springs and perch. Shafts only.

Carro paseante de estilo cuadrado; sin sombrero; asiento detras movible; suportado por dos resortes Eliptico y alcandara; varas solamente.

No. 1113. $250 to $300, Gold.

Stylish four-passenger, square-box, no-top Road-Wagon, for two horses. Very favorite style for the races. Pole only.

Carro de camino; paseante de estilo cuadrado, para cuatro passajeros; de dos caballos; un estilo favorito para carreras; lanza solamente.

Brewster & Baldwin, 786 Broadway.

LANTERN.   LADY PALMER.   BROWN DICK.   PRINCE JOHN.   NEW JERSEY.
    FLORA TEMPLE.   FLATBUSH MARE.   LANCET.

BREWSTER & BALDWIN,
MANUFACTURERS OF
FIRST CLASS CARRIAGES,
786 BROADWAY.
Next to Grace Church.]   Cor. of Tenth Street.
NEW YORK.

ILLUSTRATED CATALOGUES FURNISHED AT REQUEST.

Brewster & Baldwin, 786 Broadway.

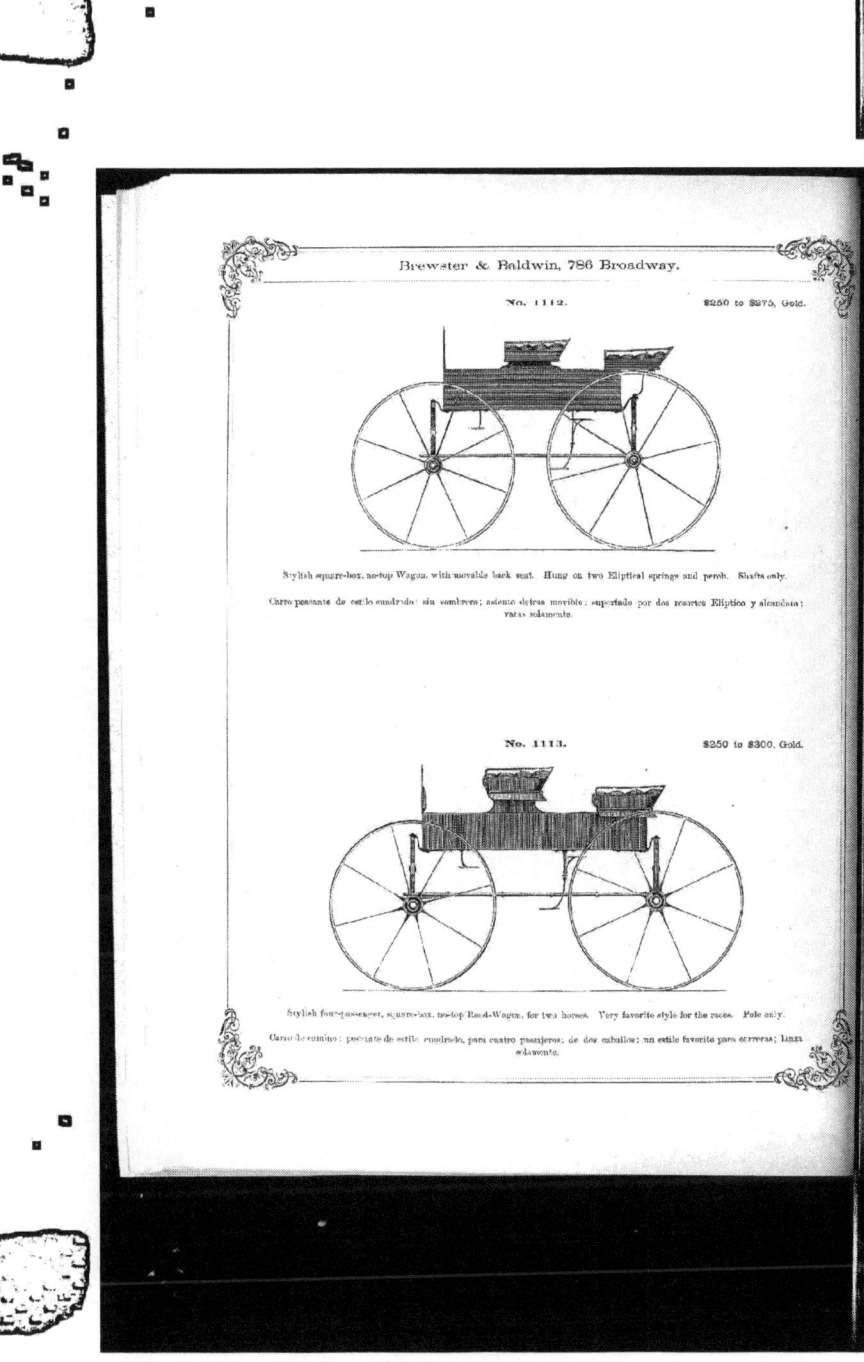

No. 1112. $250 to $275, Gold.

Stylish square-box, no-top Wagon, with movable back seat. Hung on two Eliptical springs and perch. Shafts only.

Carro paseante de estilo cuadrado; sin sombrero; asiento detras movible; suspendido por dos muelles Eliptico y alzandose; varas solamente.

No. 1113. $250 to $300, Gold.

Stylish four-passenger, square-box, no-top Road-Wagon, for two horses. Very favorite style for the races. Pole only.

Carro de camino; paseante de estilo cuadrado, para cuatro pasajeros; de dos caballos; un estilo favorito para carreras; Lanza solamente.

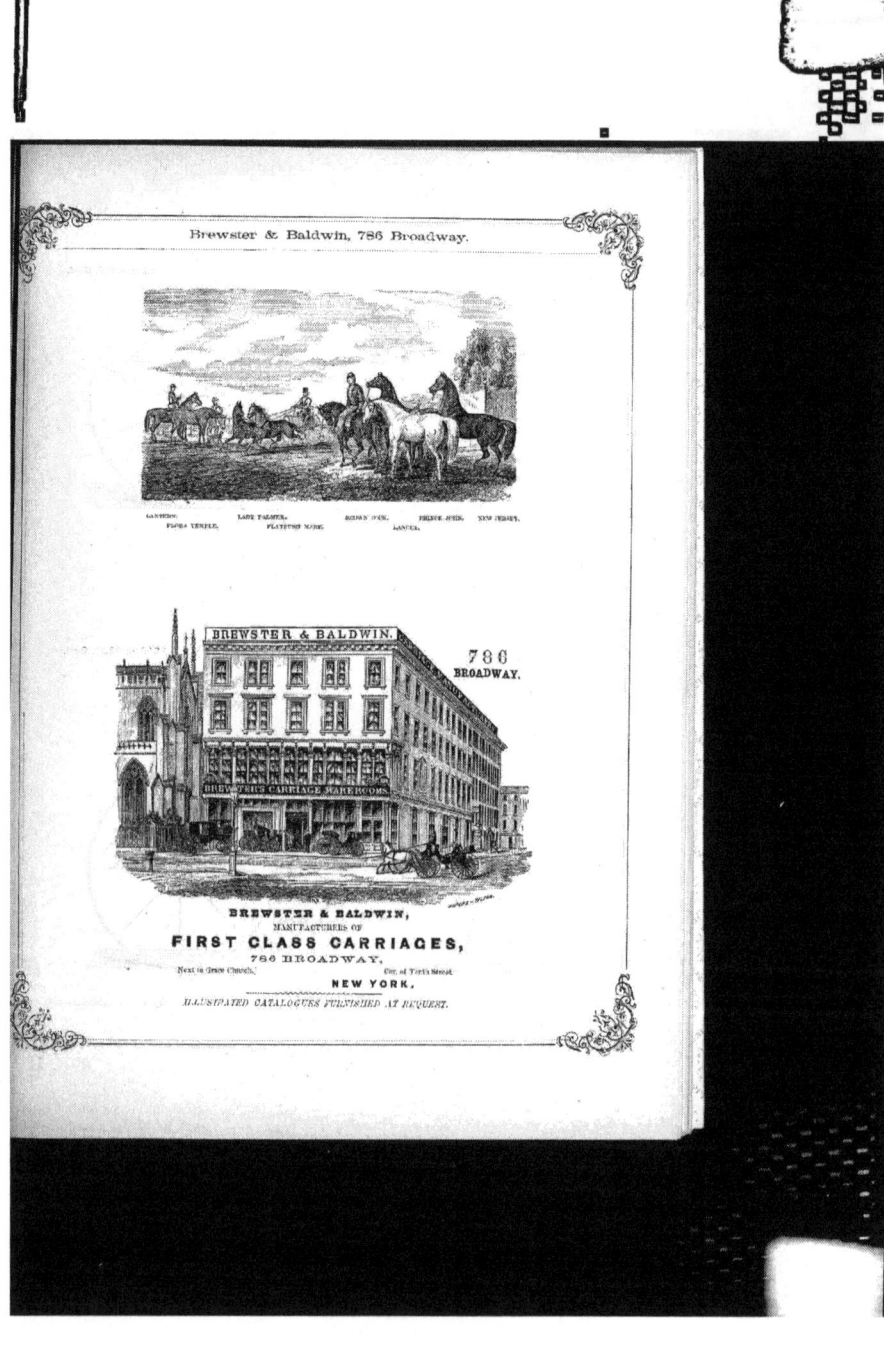

Brewster & Baldwin, 786 Broadway.

No. 1114. $75 to $125, Gold.

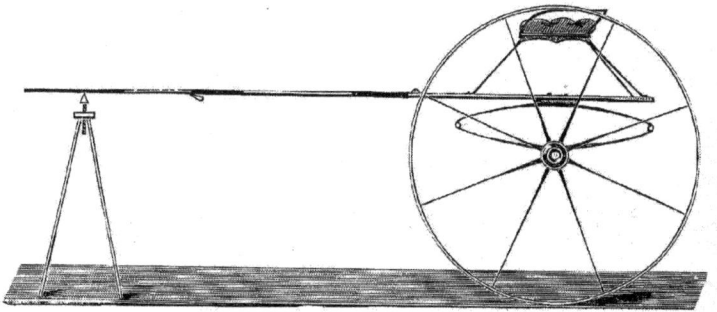

Trotting Sulky.

Dickey de trote.

No. 1115. $250 to $300, Gold.

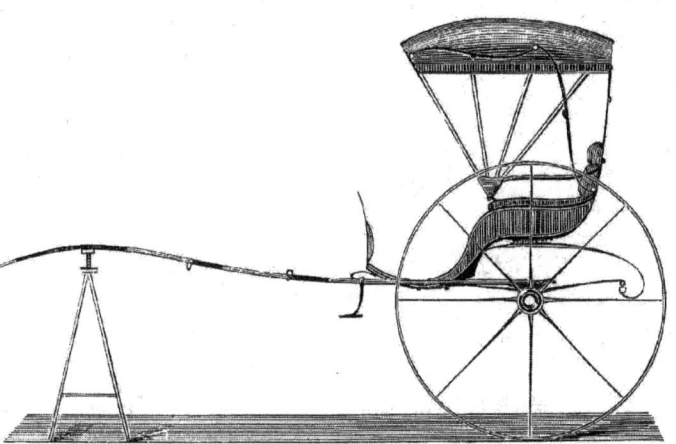

"Tampico Gig."

Gig de Tampico.

Brewster & Baldwin, 786 Broadway.

No. 1116. $140 to $150, Gold.

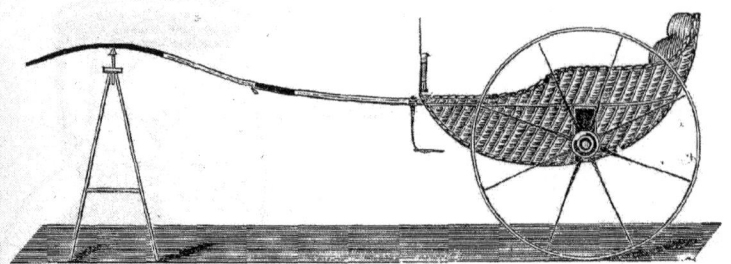

Willow "Tub." Used a great deal for nurses and children.

"Tub" de Sauce; usado para ama y niños.

No. 1117. $185 to $210, Gold.

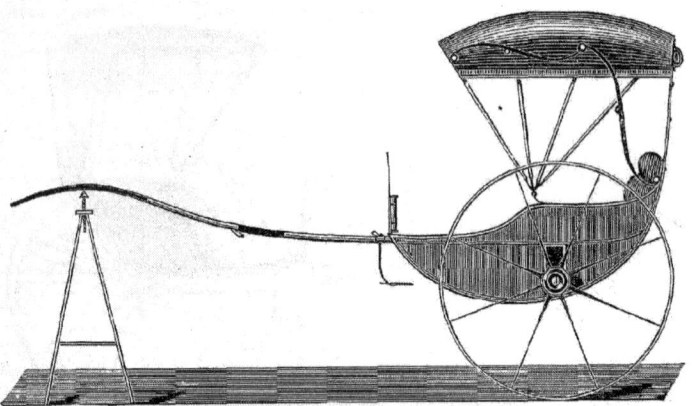

Two-wheeled, paneled "Tub," with canvas top.

"Tub" de dos ruedas de albardon, con sombrero.

Brewster & Baldwin, 786 Broadway.

No. 1118. $175 to $225, Gold.

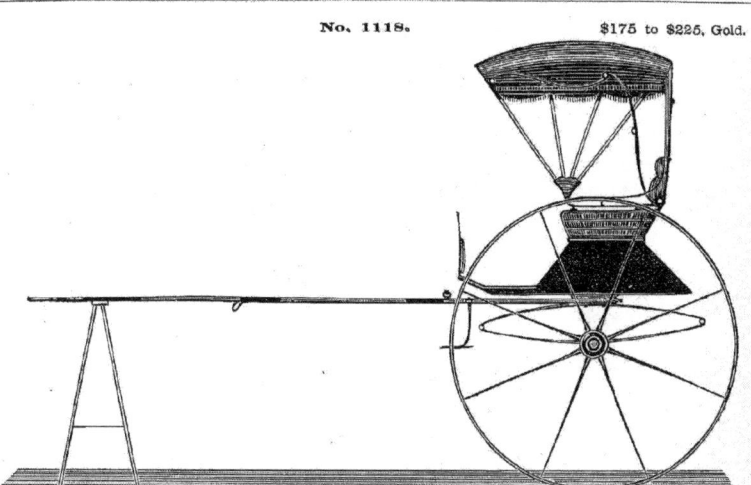

Light two-wheeled Gig, suitable for light country-work, or for business purposes, or for a physician.

Gig de dos ruedas; conveniente para ligero trabajo del campo ó de negocios o para un medico.

No. 1119. $300 to $375, Gold.

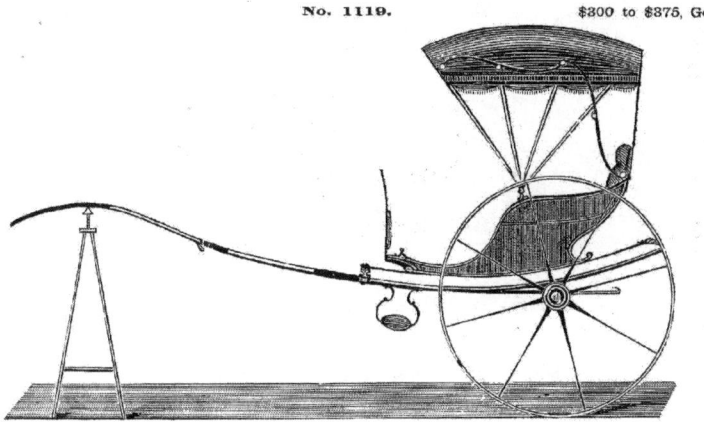

Boston Chaise.

Silla ó Chaise de Boston.

Brewster & Baldwin, 786 Broadway.

No. 1120. $400 to $550, Gold.

"French Cabriolet," with six springs.
"Cabriolet Frances," con seis resortes.

BREWSTER & BALDWIN,
MANUFACTURERS OF
FIRST CLASS CARRIAGES,
786 BROADWAY,
[Next to Grace Church.] Cor. of Tenth Street.
NEW YORK.

ILLUSTRATED CATALOGUES FURNISHED AT REQUEST.

Brewster & Baldwin, 786 Broadway.

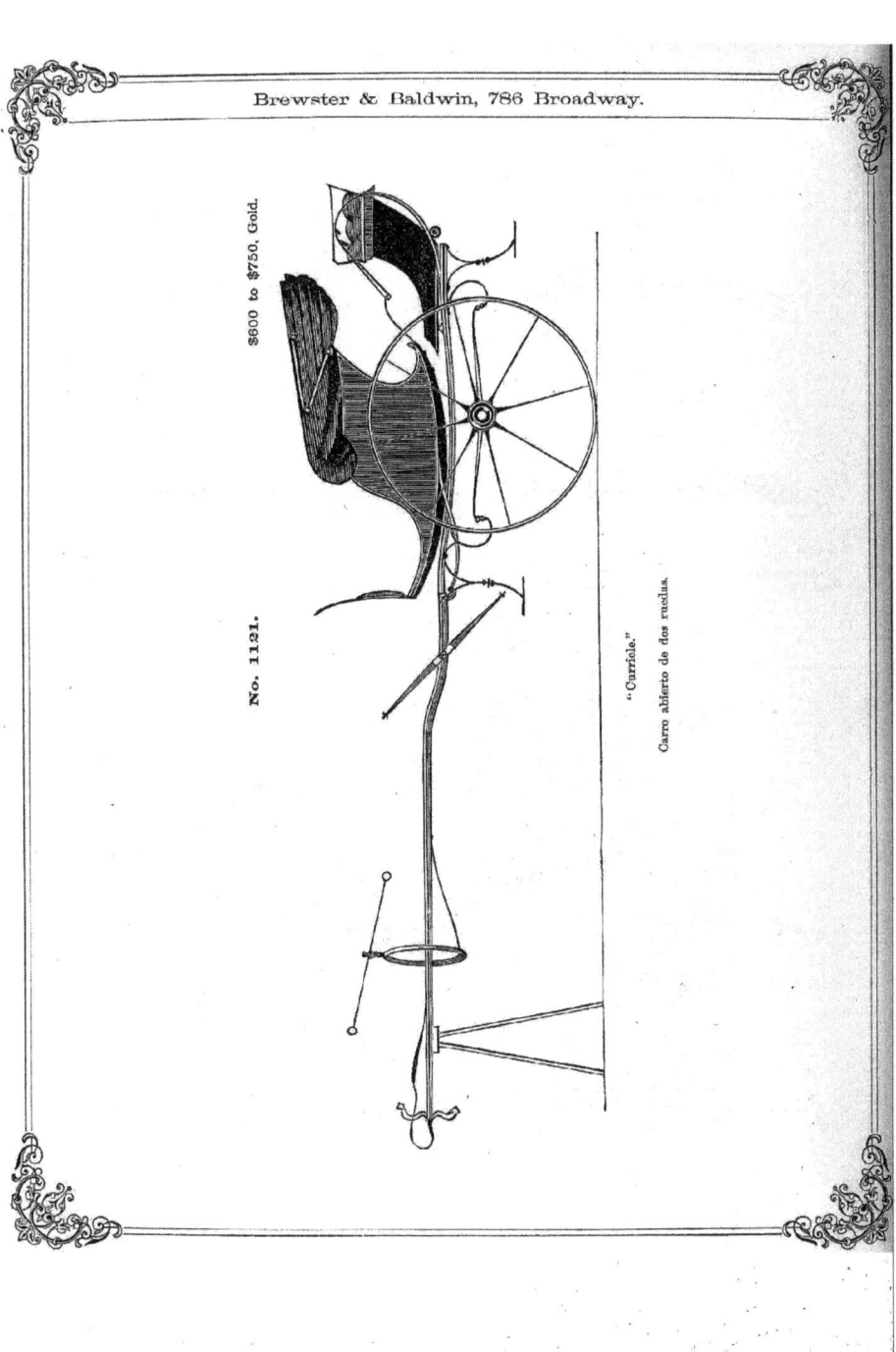

No. 1121. $600 to $750, Gold.

"Curricle."
Carro abierto de dos ruedas.

Brewster & Baldwin, 786 Broadway.

No. 1122. $300 to $400, Gold.

Barnsbury Cart; tail-board drops, and may sit back to back, or as represented in design. Light, stylish, and new pattern.

Carreton Barnsbury; tabla detras baja y se puede sentar espalda a espalda asi como es representado en el plan; ligero, al estilo y de nuevo modo.

No. 1123. $300 to $400, Gold.

Light and stylish new-style tandem Dog-Cart.

Carreton de Perro, para caballos frente en frente; ligero y al estilo.

40

Brewster & Baldwin, 786 Broadway.

No. 1124. $450 to $550, Gold.

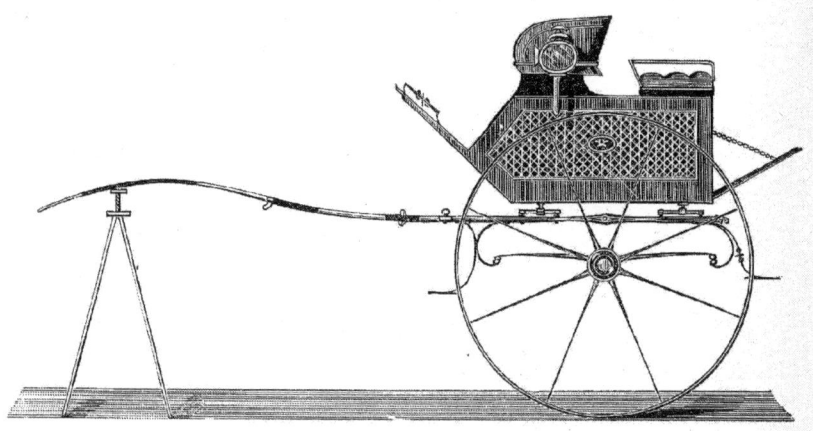

Elegant tandem "Dog-Cart."

Carreton de Perro; caballos frente en frente, elegante.

LANTERN. LADY PALMER. BROWN DICK. PRINCE JOHN. NEW JERSEY.
FLORA TEMPLE. FLATBUSH MARE. LANCET.

WOOD GIBSON,

SADDLER,

MANUFACTURER & IMPORTER OF

Saddles, Harness,

BRIDLES, WHIPS, BITS, SPURS,

&c., &c., &c., &c.

No. 793 Broadway,

Opposite Grace Church.   NEW YORK.

DANIEL F. TIEMANN.   JULIUS W. TIEMANN.   PETER C. TIEMANN.

D. F. TIEMANN & CO.,

Established, 1807,

PROPRIETORS OF THE CELEBRATED

MANHATTANVILLE COLOR WORKS

THE OLDEST COLOR MANUFACTORY IN AMERICA.

MANUFACTURERS OF

Fine Colors; Lakes, Carmine, Quicksilver, Vermillion; Fine Blues, Greens, Yellows, White-Leads, Zinc, & Varnishes; California Vermillion—a Pure Quicksilver Vermillion, fully equal to the English in every respect. We are the SOLE Manufacturers and Proprietors of this famous Brand of VERMILLION.

CARMINE,

Perfectly Pure---Especially adapted to Coach, Car, and Carriage Painting and Striping.

Cadmium Yellow, Perfect Yellow, Carmine Lakes, Munich Lakes, Chatenue and other Lakes, Chinese and Prussian Blues, Coach Black, Chrome Yellows, Chrome Greens, Patent Dryers, White Leads, Zinc Whites, and Varnishes. We make a specialty of the Fine Colors used by Coach, Car, and Carriage Manufacturers.

OFFICES: 240 PEARL STREET, & 1 BURLING SLIP,

NEW YORK.

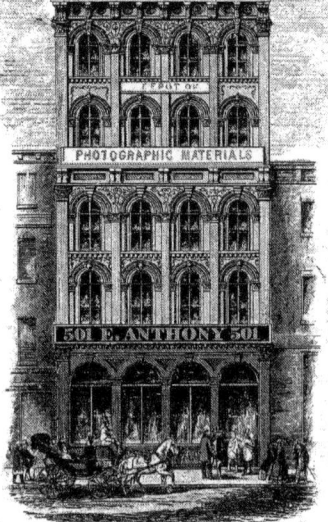

E. & H. T. ANTHONY & Co.
FABRICANTES AMERICANOS
DE MATERIALES DE FOTOGRAFIA
Albumes fotográficos. Vistas Estereoscopicos

301 Broadway, New York.
3 doors from St. Nicholas Hotel.
& 55 Rue de Bretagne, Paris.

MANUFACTURERS OF
PHOTOGRAPHIC MATERIALS
Stereoscopes
STEREOSCOPIC VIEWS & ALBUMS.

Our PHOTOGRAPHIC ALBUMS are unrivaled as to durability and finish to look of New Books.
Our assortment of CARTE DE VISITE PHOTOGRAPHS is most complete.
Our collection of imported and domestic STEREOSCOPIC VIEWS

SEE ADVERTISEMENT ON NEXT PAGE.

E. & H. T. ANTHONY & CO.,
No. 501 BROADWAY, NEW YORK,

The Oldest and Most Extensive House in the World,
Exclusively devoted to

Photographic Materials
— AND —
PHOTOGRAPHIC PUBLICATIONS,

MANUFACTURERS OF

PHOTOGRAPHIC CHEMICALS
OF SUPERIOR QUALITY.

Albumenized Paper, Varnishes, Soluble Cotton, for Colodion, Gilt and Fancy Frames, Cases of Velvet and Leather, Passe-portens, &c., &c., &c.

An extensive stock always on hand of everything pertaining to the PHOTOGRAPHIC ART, including the largest assortment in America of

Stereoscopic Views and Albums.

E. & H. T. ANTHONY & CO.,
501 BROADWAY, NUEVA YORK,
No. 55 RUE DE BRETAGNE, PARIS,

Establecidos 25 años ha,

FABRICANTES EN GRAN ESCALA DE

MATERIALES DE FOTOGRAFIA.

La fama de nuestros artículos se extiende por todo Sur America y por las Antillas, y no necesitamos por consiguiente de hablar aquí de ella.

LO QUE NOS PROPONEMOS CON ESTE AVISO es llamar la atencion al hecho de haber establecido una oficina en el

No. 55 Rue de Bretagne, Paris,

desde donde podemos proporcionar á nuestros parroquianos todos los artículos que necesiten de Inglaterra, Francia, y Alemania, á precios razonables.

Nuestros artículos Americanos se seguirán embarcando en Nueva York, como hasta ahára.

Las remesas de fondos deben dirigirse á la casa de Nueva York, y pueden hacerse por medio de libranzas sobre Nueva York, Londres ó Paris.

N.B.—Desempeñarémos ademas toda órden que se nos dirija por artículos extraños á nuestra profesion, ofreciendo prestarles la mayor atencion y cargar los mismos precios de fábrica.

VIEW OF THE SCOVILL MFG. CO'S WORKS.

Scovill Manufacturing Co.

MANUFACTURERS
— OF —

Sheet and Roll Brass,
German Silver,
Brass and Copper Wire,
Silver Plated Ware & Metal,

Brass Butt Hinges,
Metal Lamps & Trimmings,
Metal Blanks Cut to Order.
Coal Oil Burners,

Gilt, Lasting, Brocade & Fancy Dress Buttons
IN EVERY VARIETY.

Particular attention given to Special Designs for Livery, Military, Naval, School, and other Metal Buttons.

Manufacturers, Importers, & Dealers in every Description of

PHOTOGRAPHIC GOODS,
Etc., Etc., Etc., Etc., Etc.

Agents for Jerome's celebrated 8 day & Calendar Clocks.

MANUFACTORIES:
Waterbury, Connecticut,
New Haven, Connecticut.

AGENCIES:
4 Beekman Street, New York,
134 Federal St., Boston,
73 Bold St., Liverpool, G.B.

Compañía Manufacturera
— DE —
SCOVILL,
FABRICANTE DE

Planchas y cilindros de Bronce
Plata Alemana,
Alambre de Cobre y de Bronce,
Artículos Plateados,

Quicios de Bronce,
Lámparas de Metal y sus accesorios,
Quemadores para aceite de Carbon,

Piezas de Metal Cortados á la Orden.

Botones Dorados, para Brocados y Vestidos
DE CAPRICHO DE TODAS CLASES.

Se prestá átencion particular á los diseños especiales de Botones de Metal para Libreas, Uniformes Militares y Navales, Escuelas, y otras Clases.

Fabrica, Importa y Comercia en toda Clase de
EFECTOS PARA FOTOGRAFIA
Etc., Etc., Etc., Etc.
ES AGENTE DE LOS
Famosos Relojes de Jerome, con ocho dias de Cuerda y Calendario,

FABRICAS:
Waterbury, Connecticut,
New Haven, Connecticut,

AGENCIAS:
4 Beekman Street, New York,
134 Federal St., Boston,
73 Bold St., Liverpool, G.B.

E. CLEAVE.   AUG. C. ROGERS.

Cleave & Rogers,

STEAM

BOOK & JOB PRINTERS

PUBLISHERS,

58 Liberty & 37 Nassau Sts., N.Y.

In Press, and soon to be Published,

THE HISTORY OF NEW YORK CITY

— FROM THE —

Discovery to the Present Day,

By WM. L. STONE,

Author of the Life and times of Sir William Johnson, Bart.; Life and Writings of the late Colonel William L. Stone, &c., &c. &c.

CLEAVE & ROGERS, Publishers.

W. GIBSON,

Saddler,

HARNESS

AND PATENT

TRAVELING TRUNK

MANUFACTURER,

Importer of Fine London Saddles, Bridles, Holly Whips, Bits, Spurs, &c.,

No. 793 BROADWAY,

Opposite Grace Church,

New York.

PARIS EXHIBITION, 1867.

First Grand Prize! Highest Award!

CROSS OF THE LEGION OF HONOR
—AND—
GOLD MEDAL.

Chickering & Sons Triumphant!

The Highest Recompense over all Competition at the UNIVERSAL EXPOSITION, PARIS, 1867, was awarded to

CHICKERING & SONS,

FOR THE DIFFERENT STYLES OF
PIANOS EXHIBITED BY THEM.

They were the only Exhibitors of PIANOS who received the double recompense of THE CROSS OF THE LEGION OF HONOR AND GOLD MEDAL. This award distinctly and fully classifies the CHICKERING PIANO as First in the Order of Merit. Pamphlets containing Official Certificates and Extracts, giving undeniable proof of the above statements, can be had at our Ware-Rooms,

No. 652 BROADWAY, NEW YORK,
—AND—
246 WASHINGTON ST., BOSTON.

CHICKERING & SONS have been awarded Sixty-five First Prize Medals over all competitors for the superiority of their manufacture, exhibited by them at the different Fairs in this Country and in Europe. Also, the most flattering testimonials from the leading Artists in the Profession.

LUNT & HOWELLS,

IMPORTERS OF

Carriage Cloths, Carpets,

CURTAIN SILKS,

COTELINES AND SATINS,

14 WARREN STREET,

New York.

WM. BOSTON.   F. J. SCHMID.

BOSTON & SCHMID,
MANUFACTURERS OF
Coach Lace, Fringe, Tassels,
AND
SPEAKING-TUBES;
ALSO, MANUFACTURERS OF
LADIES' DRESS TRIMMINGS;
CONSTANTLY ON HAND,
Rubber Tubing for Speaking-Tubes,
699 BROADWAY, CORNER FOURTH STREET,
(Entrance on Fourth Street,) **NEW YORK.**

GODDARD'S BURRING MACHINE WORKS,
SECOND AVENUE, Cor. 22d STREET,
OFFICE, 3 BOWLING GREEN, NEW YORK,

MANUFACTURE THE
PATENT MESTIZO WOOL BURRING PICKERS,
For Opening, Picking, Dusting and Burring MESTIZO and all other medium to fine Foreign and Domestic WOOLS, and Cleaning Waste.
PATENT WORSTED WOOL BURRING PICKERS,
For Opening, Picking, Dusting and Burring WORSTED, CARPET, DELAINE, and other Coarse Foreign and Domestic WOOLS.
PATENT STEEL RING AND SOLID PACKING BURRING MACHINES
SINGLE & DOUBLE, FOR FIRST BREAKERS OF WOOL-CARDING MACHINES.
Steel-Ring Feed-Rolls, with Patent Adjustable Spring-Boxes.
SHAKE WILLOWS, with Blowers for Opening and Dusting Wool.
WASTE DUSTERS. KAYSER'S PATENT GESSNER OILS.
Prompt attention given to all inquiries and orders addressed to
C. L. GODDARD, No. 3 Bowling Green, N. Y.

FABRICA DE MAQUINAS DE GODDARD PARA LIMPIAR LANAS,
SEGUNDA AVENIDA, ESQUINA A LA CALLE 22,
Oficina, **3 BOWLING GREEN, NUEVA YORK,**
FABRICA EL
LIMPIADOR PRIVILEGIADO PARA LANA MESTIZA,
El cual abre, escoje, desempolva y limpia la LANA MESTIZA, y todas las otras clases m alinnas á finas extranjeras y del pais, y limpia las desperdicios.
LIMPIADORES PRIVILEGIADOS DE LANAS PARA ESTAMBRE,
Los cuales abrir, escojen desempolvan y limpian las LANAS para ESTAMBRE, ALFOMBRA, y cualquier otra clase de lana ordinaria, extraajera ó del pais.
MAQUNIAS LIMPIADORAS sólidas y con avos de acero, dobles y sencillas, para cardadores de lana;
Varillas alimentadoras de acero, con cajas de muelle privilegiadas; Sacudidores con soplador para abrir y desempolvar lana. Desempolvadores de desechos. Se atiende prontamente á todas los informes que se pidan y á las órdenes que se dirijan á
C. L. GODDARD, 3 Bowling Green, N. Y.

A. CHRISTIAN,
Manufacturer of Christian's
Patent Spring Rocking Horses,

EVERY DESCRIPTION OF
CHILDREN'S CARRRIAGES, PERAMBULATORS,
Gigs, Cabs, Propellers, Rocking-Horses, Sleighs, Sleds, &c.

Have also constantly on hand an assortment of Wheelbarrows, Wagons, Toy Carts, &c., at lowest cash prices, to which we invite the attention of the trade.

WAREHOUSE, 65 MAIDEN LANE,
Manufactory, 87, 89, 91, 93 & 95 Mangin St., New York.

A. CHRISTIAN,
Fabricante de los
Caballos Mecedores de Resorte Patente de Christian,
Y TODA CLASE DE

Carruajes para Niños, Perambulantes Calesas,

CARROS, MOTORES CABALLOS, MECEDORES TRINEOS, &c. &c.

Tienen ademas un surtido de Angarillas, precios bajos, y dignos de  Wagones, Carretillas para muñecas, &c., a la atencion del comercio.

ALMACEN, No. 65 MAIDEN LANE,
Fábrica, 87, 89, 91, 93, y 95 Mangin St., Nueva York.

J. E. Condict & Co.,

32 Warren and 102 Chambers Streets, N. Y.

WHOLESALE

Saddlery Harness,

AND

SADDLERY, HARDWARE,

Trunks, Bags, Valises, &c., &c.

This well-known house, having been exclusively in the Southern and Southwestern Trade for over Fifty Years, is enabled to offer the largest and best assorted stock of goods in their line to be found in New York.

Great inducements will at all times be offered **CASH AND FIRST-CLASS TIME BUYERS.**

Factories,
Newark, N. J.

Catálogo de los Libros Publicados
—POR—
D. APPLETON Y COMPAÑÍA,
Libreros-Editores, Nueva York.
CON LOS PRECIOS EN ORO DE LOS E. U.

ASTA BURUAGA. Diccionario Jeográfico de la República de Chile. Por Francisco Solano Asta Buraga. Un tomo de 421 páginas, en 12°. $9.00.

ALFABETO EN PIEZAS. Juguete para Niños. Es una cajita de seis pulgadas de alto, que encierra 27 piezas cúbicas perfectamente cortadas é iguales, cada una en sus seis caras contiene una letra del alfabeto; tres palabras que empiezan con dicha letra, un fino grabado de colores y un número en cifra y en letra. Cada cajita 75.

BELLO. Compendio de la Gramática Castellana, de Andrés Bello, escrito para uso de las escuelas de la América Española. Por J. Arnaldo Marqués. Un tomo de 135 páginas, en 18°. 37½.

BURNOUF. Elementos de Gramática Latina, Extractados del Método para Estudiar la Lengua Latina, por J. L. Burnouf. Traducido del Francés al Castellano por Juan Vicente Gonzalez. Un tomo de 164 páginas, en 12°. 75.

BUTLER. El Maestro de Inglés, ó Libro de Frases Familiares. Por Francisco Butler. Un tomo de 202 páginas, en 18°. 50.

CARREÑO. Manual de Urbanidad y Buenas Maneras, para uso de la juventud de ambos sexos. Un tomo de 322 páginas, en 18°. 50.

CARREÑO. Compendio del Manual de Urbanidad y buenas maneras, de Manuel Antonio Carreño. Arreglado para uso de las escuelas de ambos sexos. Un tomo de 120 páginas, en 18°. 37½.

CERVANTES. El Ingenioso Hidalgo Don Quijote de la Mancha, con el texto corregido y anotado por el señor Ochoa. Un tomo de 695 páginas, en 12°. 1 25.

CERVANTES. El Ingenioso Hidalgo Don Quijote de la Mancha segun el texto corregido y anotado por el señor Ochoa. Edicion de lujo con catorce láminas y retrato de Cervantes. Un tomo de 695 páginas, en 8°. cantos dorados, 3 50.

COE. Cartones de Dibujo para las Escuelas, en diez partes. Por Coe. Cada parte, 30.

CORNELL. Cartones de Cornell para el Estudio y práctica del dibujo de mapas. Designados para acompañar cualquiera geografía. Un juego de 13 mapas. 50.

CORNELL. Mapas de Cornell. Juego de 13 Mapas mudos con los lugares marcados por números en vez de nombres. 12 00.

CORNELL. Una Clave de los Mapas Mudos de Cornell. Designada para el uso del profesor. Un tomo para 59 páginas, en 12°. 50.

CUENTOS ILUMINADOS PARA NIÑOS. Coleccion de diez libritos para recreo de la infancia. Con graciosas láminas de colores.

EL GATO BANDIDO, PANTOMICA, Y JUAN CHUNGUERO, LA POBRE VIEJECITA,
EL RINACUAJO PASEADOR, LA VÉNUS DORMIDA, SIMON EL BONITO,
LA UNICIENTA, Ó EL ZAPATITO DE VIDRIO, ALADINO, Ó LA LAMPARA MARAVILLOSA, LOS TRES GATITOS, Y LA CENA DEL ZORRO,
EL PARDILLO, LOS TRES OSOS, NENE PULGARITA.

Doce libritos en paquetes surtidos, la docena, 50.

DE BEHM. Libro de Frases Inglesas y Españolas. Por E. M. de Behm. Un tomo de 88 páginas, en 18°. 30.

DE MARLIENA. Compendio de la Historia Antigua, ó Historia de los principales pueblos de la antigüedad. Hasta la muerte de Carlomagno. Escrita en Inglés, y traducida al Castellano, por A. R. De Marliena. Un tomo de 232 páginas, en 18°. 50.

DICCIONARIO MERCANTIL, en Inglés, Francés, y Español, por D. L. de Veitelle. Un tomo de 305 páginas, en 12°. 1 75.

DUSSELDORFF. Perlas de la Galería de Dusseldorff. fotografías originales por A. A. Turner. Reproducidas (por la primera vez bajo la direccion de E. Fyrdham. Un tomo en folio grande, conteniendo 32 fotografías elegantemente encuadernado en tafilete. 9 00.

ELEMENTOS DE LA HISTORIA UNIVERSAL, para uso de las escuelas Hispano-Americanas. Un tomo de 431 páginas, en 8°. 2 50.

EN LENGUAGE DE LAS FLORES Y DE LAS FRUTAS con algunos Emblemas de las Piedras y las Colores. Un bonito muy atractivo de 146 páginas, en 18°. 50.

FLORIAN. Guillermo Tell, Libertador de la Suiza y Andres Hofer, el "Tell" del Tirol. Por Florian. Con la Vida del Autor. Un bonito tomo de 251 páginas, con grabados. 1 00.

GRANDE. Compendio de Aritmética Elemental para la Instruction Primaria, por M. P. Grande. Un tomo de 60 páginas, en 12°. 15.

HISTORIETAS MORALES para la Infancia. Escritas en Inglés, por S. G. Goodrich, autor de las "Conversaciones de Parley", etc. Un tomo de 332 páginas, con dice y seis bonitas láminas. 1 50.

LE SAGE. Historia de Gil Blas de Santillana, publicada en Francés por A. R. Le Sage, traducida al Castellano por el Padre Isla. Un tomo en 13°. 1 25.

LIBRO PRIMARIO DE LOS NIÑOS. Cartilla adornada con láminas iluminadas. Por tomo de 14 páginas. 8°. La docena, 1 50.

LIBRO PRIMARIO DE ORTOGRAFIA, designado particularmente para uso de las escuelas de primeras letras. Un tomo de 104 páginas en 12°. 37½.

LOS MISERABLES. Novela por Victor Hugo. Traducida del original Frances al Castellano por D. José Segundo Flores. Dos tomos 8°, encuadernados en tela. 3 00.

MANDEVIL. Libro Primario para uso de los Niños por el Doctor Enrique Mandevil. Un tomo de 95 páginas, con láminas, en 12°. Nueva edicion, enteramente corregida, y con grabados nuevos. 25.

MANDEVIL. Libro Segundo por el Doctor Enrique Mandevil. Un tomo de 118 páginas, con láminas, en 12°. 37½.

MANDEVIL. Libro Tercero de Lectura. Un tomo en 12°, constando de mas de 250 páginas. 50.

MARSH. Curso Practico de Teneduria de Libros. Partida sencilla. Por C. C. Marsh, contador. Un tomo de 144 páginas, en 8°. 1 50.

MARSH. La Ciencia de la Teneduría de Libros, bien calculada para enseñar completamente la Teoría y la Práctica de la partida doble. Por C. C. Marsh, contador. Un tomo de 196 páginas, en 8°. 1 50.

MARSH. Juegos de Libros en blanco. Para la Practica de la Teneduría. Seis libros componen un juego. Cada juego, 1 25.

MUÑECAS de PAPEL Seis Clases; dos de cada una; á saber:

ANITA GOMEZ, ROSITA, LOLA,
PANCHITA, LA SEÑORA TOMAS PULGAR, EL GENERAL TOMAS PULGAR.

En paquetes surtidos. La docena, 1 50.

NUEVO TESORO de Chistes, Maximas, Proverbios, Reflexiones Morales, Historias, Cuentos y Leyendas. Extractados de las obras de los mejores autores Ingleses y Americanos. Traducido al Castellano por Simon Camacho. Un tomo de 271 páginas, en 12°. 1 00.

OLLENDORFF. Método para aprender á leer escribir y hablar el Inglés, segun el sistema de Ollendorff. Por Ramon Palenzuela y Juan de la C. Carreño. Un tomo de 436 páginas, en 14°. 1 00.

OLLENDORFF. Clave de los Ejercicios del Método para aprender á leer, escribir y hablar el Inglés, segun el sistema de Ollendorff. Por Ramon Palenzuela y Juan de la C. Carreño. Un tomo de 211 páginas, en 12°. 75.

OLLENDORFF. Un Método para aprender á leer, escribir y hablar el Frances segun el sistema de Ollendorff. Por Teodoro Simonné. Un tomo de 341 páginas, en 12°. 1 00.

OLLENDORFF. Clave de los Ejercicios del Método para aprender á leer, escribir y hablar el Frances segun el sistema de Ollendorff. Por Teodoro Simonné. Un tomo de 83 páginas, en 12°. 75.

OTIS. Estudios sobre los Animales, con instrucciones para el uso del lapiz de plomo y de crayon. Por F. N. Otis, A. M. Un tomo. 2 50.

OTIS. Lecciones Faciles de Paisaje con instrucciones para el uso del lapiz de plomo y de crayon. Por F. N. Otis, A. M. Un tomo. 230.

ORTIZ. Principios Fundamentales sobre Educacion Popular y los nuevos Métodos de Enseñanza. Por Pedro Ortiz. Un tomo de 288 páginas, en 12°. 1 50.

ORTIZ. Principios Elementales de Física Experimental y Aplicada, incluyendo la Meteorologia, y la Climatologia. Por Pedro P. Ortiz. Un tomo de 507 páginas y 164 grabados, en 12°. 1 50.

PAEZ. Libro Segundo de Geografía Descriptiva, arreglada a seguir al Primero de Smith. Adornado con doze grandes mapas y mas de 100 grabados que sirven para mejor inteligencia del texto. Edicion enteramente nueva, corregida y aumentada conforme a los últimos datos estadísticos y cambios políticos, arreglada al uso de las escuelas Hispano-Americanas. Por D. Ramon Paez. Un tomo de 90 páginas grandes. 1 25.

PERKINS. Lecciones de Aritmética Elemental, basadas en el nuevo sistema mental y práctico adoptado en las principales escuelas de los Estados Unidos. Por Jorge R. Perkins. Un tomo de 163 páginas, en 18°. 37½.

QUACKENBUS. Historia Ilustrada de los Estados Unidos y paises adyacentes de América, desde los tiempos mas remotos hasta el presente. Por G. P. Quackenbus, Maestro en Artes. Traducida al Castellano por A. de Tornos. Un tomo de 247 páginas, conteniendo muchos mapas y grabados. 1 80.

ADVERTENCIA.—Las obras que anteceden se hallan de venta en todas las principales librerías de las Antillas, Méjico, y la América del Sur. A los que deseen comprar por sus cantidades, y remitan una orden á los editores-libreros, cuyo importe no baje de cien pesos y venga acompañada con la remision de lo que importe, se le hará un descuento de veinticinco por ciento de los precios adjuntos.

Para que les órdenes sean atendidas y prontamente despachadas, deben venir acompañadas con el dinero ó que acciende su importe.

Los libros se venden á los precios citados en oro, únicamente por exportación de los Estados Unidos.

WILLIAM TILDEN,
WILLIAM T. BLODGETT.
ESTABLISHED, 1830.

William Tilden & Nephew,

MANUFACTURERS OF

VARNISHES AND JAPANS,

EXPRESSLY FOR

Coach-Makers & Railway-Car Builders,

252 Pearl Street,   **NEW YORK.**

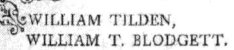

The attention of CONSUMERS and DEALERS is called to this LIST, and to the testimony of several of the best Coach and Carriage Manufacturers in this city, who have used and thoroughly tested our different grades of COACH VARNISHES. The long experience of our house, and the confidence reposed in it by the manufacturers and dealers of the country for the last 38 YEARS, has induced us to give special attention, and to spare no expense, in perfecting the qualities of our COACH VARNISHES to meet the requirements of the best COACH MANUFACTURERS in the UNITED STATES. For the past FIVE YEARS we have devoted one of our factories exclusively to the manufacturing of COACH VARNISHES and JAPANS, and from our large stock, constantly on hand, we are able to ensure uniformity in quality. All our COACH VARNISHES are fully tested by a practical coach painter, to determine their drying and wearing qualities, before they are distributed to our customers. An impartial trial will convince any unprejudiced party of the superiority of our COACH VARNISHES.

IMPERIAL WEARING BODY.
Used for finishing best Coach Bodies and Railway Cars. Is of light shade, very durable, and retains a brilliant gloss, works easy under the brush, sets free from dust in fifteen hours, and dries hard in three days.

ELASTIC CARRIAGE.
For finishing running parts of Carriages. It is very elastic, and pale in color, dries readily, and retains its brilliancy equal to any varnish.

HARD DRYING BODY.
Intended for first coats on Coach Bodies and Railway Cars. Is very transparent, works freely, dries hard, and rubs well without sweating, leaving a smooth, bright surface for finishing with our Imperial Wearing Body, or other varnish.

CARRIAGE RUBBING.
Used for first coats on running parts of Carriages, dries hard in twenty-four hours, and will not sweat in rubbing.

NO. 1 COACH BODY.
Expressly adapted for finishing with one coat, and is much liked for general Coach and Carriage work. Is of heavy body, bright gloss, and dries quickly.

NO. 1 CARRIAGE.
This is designed for Wagons, running parts of Carriages, and ordinary outside work, and is the quickest drying of our Coach Varnishes.

LOCOMOTIVE.
For Engines, or other much exposed work. It is very transparent, and dries hard in twelve hours.

COACHMAKERS' DRYING BROWN JAPAN.
Celebrated for its drying and binding qualities. Is light in color, works free, and incorporates readily with oil.

GOLD SIZE.
For Gilding purposes. Sets quick, and holds the tack for three hours, giving time to lay Gold Leaf.

ENAMEL CARRIAGE-TOP DRESSING.
Gives a brilliant surface and elasticity to the Leather, and is admitted to be a very superior article. Applied with a brush.

BLACK JAPAN (SELF-DRYING).
To protect all kinds of iron for coach work. Has a brilliant lustre.

INSIDE CAR FINISHING.
For interiors of Railway Cars. Gives a clear, brilliant, and lasting surface. Dries in ten hours.

The following Testimonials are from some of the most prominent Coach Manufacturers in this city:

65 East 29th St., New York, Feb. 13, 1868.
Messrs. WILLIAM TILDEN & NEPHEW:
Gentlemen—For some time past we have used your Body and Carriage Varnishes, and take pleasure in recommending them to the trade as superior in all respects. Your obedient servants,
BREWSTER & BALDWIN.

New York, February 13, 1868.
Messrs. WILLIAM TILDEN & NEPHEW:
Gentlemen—Having thoroughly tested your Finishing Varnish for Carriage parts, we cheerfully recommend it to the use of those requiring such an article. Yours respectfully,
DUSENBURY & VAN DUSER.

Cor. 3d Ave. and 125th St., N. Y., Feb. 15, 1868.
Messrs. WILLIAM TILDEN & NEPHEW:
Dear Sirs—After long continued use of your Finishing and Rubbing Varnishes for Coach Bodies, we have no hesitation in recommending them to the trade as superior in every respect to any others we have tested; and we may also add that your Brown Japan is equal to the best we have ever used.
Yours respectfully, ADAMS & CONE.

New York, January 20, 1868.
Messrs. WILLIAM TILDEN & NEPHEW:
Gentlemen—We have used, and are using, the Imperial Wearing Body and Elastic Carriage Varnishes of your manufacture, and take pleasure in recommending them as being much superior to those of any other American Manufacture. We are also using your Hard Drying Body Varnish and Brown Japan, and find them as good as any we have used.
Yours, very respectfully, CORBETT & SCHARCK.

Nos. 94, 96, 98, 100, and 102, East 31st St., New York, Feb. 14, 1868.
Messrs. WILLIAM TILDEN & NEPHEW:
Sirs—I have been using your Varnishes and Japans for the past year, and take pleasure in saying I believe them to be as good as any in use.
Yours truly, R. M. STIVERS.

1464 Broadway, New York, Jan. 27, 1868.
Messrs. WILLIAM TILDEN & NEPHEW:
Gentlemen—We find, from use, that your Imperial Wearing Body and Elastic Carriage Varnishes of your own manufacture are as good, and in some respects better, than any similar goods in the market. We also recommend your Hard Drying Body Varnish and Brown Japan to be as good as any now in use. Very respectfully, yours,
BROWN & GODWIN.

HEROY & MARRENNER,

Nos. 90 and 92 Beekman Street, cor. Cliff,

NEW YORK,

IMPORTERS OF

Coach and Window Glass,

CONSISTING OF

CHANCE'S ENGLISH CRYSTAL PLATE,

(About 1-8th of an inch thick.)

AND

Chance's Double Thickness Crystal Sheet,

(The next best to Plate,) for

Coaches and Rail-Road Cars.

English Polished and Rough Plate Glass.

CHANCE'S ENGLISH GRYSTAL SHEET,

Single, Extra, and Double Thickness for Stores, Dwellings, Green-Houses, Pictures, and Photographers' Use;

Also,

MICROSCOPIC, OPTICAL, COLORED, STAINED, ORNAMENTAL, AND POLISHED CROWN GLASS; FLUTED OR CORRUGATED GLASS FOR GREEN-HOUSES, SKY-LIGHTS, AND DOOR-PANELS; GLAZIERS' DIAMONDS.

AGENTS FOR

Chance Brothers & Co., Birmingham,

AND THE

LONDON AND MANCHESTER PLATE GLASS CO.,

Sutton, near St. Helens, England.

Risks of transportation cannot be taken. Goods are packed in a careful manner, and delivered at the owners' risk and expense.

Claims for deficiency must be made within Three Days of Receipt of Goods, or not allowed.

Insurance against breakage on Polished Plate Glass effected when desired.

A. S. THORP & CO.,

Importers and Wholesale Dealers in

UPHOLSTERY GOODS,

Manufacturers of Furniture Springs,

AND

SOLE AGENTS

OF THE

Manchester Gimp Co.,

163 WILLIAM STREET,

A. S. THORP,
JAS. H. THORP,
JOHN C. HILL.

NEW YORK.

Stone and Barron,
PRINTERS,
No. 98 NASSAU STREET,
New York.

Wm. L. Stone,   J. T. Barron.

Catalogues of every description printed in good style. *Vide* THIS ONE.
Also every description of Job and Book Work.

Grafton Mineral Paint,

SOLD BY THE PRINCIPAL ENGLISH VARNISH MANUFACTURERS AS

English Filling-in;

For Coaches, Carriages, &c.

This Paint makes a finer surface than anything yet discovered, and is polished with very little labor.

Price per Barrel of 300 lbs., ... $6 00.

ONLY MANUFACTURED BY

Daniel Bidwell,

Importer and Dealer in Paints, Oils, &c.,

254 Pearl Street, New York.

Charles Weeks,

Carriage Builders'

Furnishing Warehouse,

No. 80 Fourth Avenue,

New York.

JAMES HOW, President.   B. W. HOW, Secretary.

THE UNION WHITE-LEAD MANUFACTURING CO.

No. 26 BURLING SLIP, NEW YORK.

We offer to the Trade and Consumers our well-known and approved

WHITE-LEADS,

Both DRY and GROUND IN OIL, RED-LEAD, LITHARGE, ORANGE MINERAL, manufactured by us from selected Metallic Lead, and, in all essential qualities, equal to the best English Lead.

CARRIAGE LEAD.

We prepare for Carriage Manufacturers a WHITE-LEAD, branded as above, for Body or Foundation Color, which dries quick, hard, and tough; is not liable to crack, and requires *no other preparation for use* than to be thinned with Spirits Turpentine. It has been used, and is highly approved, by first-class Carriage Manufacturers in this city, New Haven, and elsewhere. We are permitted to refer to

Messrs. BREWSTER & BALDWIN,   MINER, STEVENS & CO.,
And many others.

WE ARE ALSO DEALERS IN

LINSEED-OIL, SPIRITS TURPENTINE, &c., &c.

Quotations cheerfully furnished, and Orders promptly executed. Address,

The Union White-Lead Manufacturing Co.,

P. O. BOX, 2234,   **NEW YORK.**

ARCHER, PANCOAST & CO.

Manufacturers
OF
GAS-FIXTURES
AND
Lamps
OF
EVERY DESCRIPTION.

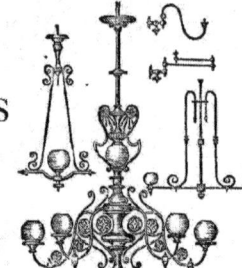

Warerooms
AND
MANUFACTORY,
Nos. 9, 11, and 13
MERCER STREET,
New York.

The attention of Buyers is called to their extensive assortment, comprising a great variety of
PATTERNS OF NEW AND BEAUTIFUL DESIGNS,
Finished in the MOST ARTISTIC STYLE, and which are offered at *VERY LOW PRICES.*

Se llama la atencion de los comisionistas y otras personas hácia la considerable existencia de útiles para gas, Lámparas de aceite de carbon, Candelabros, etc.; todo acabado á estilo artistico, y vendido á los parroquianos á los precios mas ínfimos. ARCHER, PANCOAST y Ca.,
Nos. 9, 11, & 13 Mercer Street, Nueva York.

C. A. ZOEBISCH & SONS,
Importers of, and Wholesale Dealers in,
MUSICAL INSTRUMENTS, STRINGS, &c., &c.
No. 46 Maiden Lane, New York.
Depot of C. F. MARTIN & Co.'s celebrated Guitars, acknowledged to be the best in the World.

We have received testimonials from the following players, who are considered the best soloists known:—

MADAME DE GONI,		MR. S. DE LA COVA,
MR. J. B. COUPA,	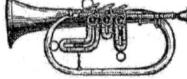	MR. CHAS. DE JANON,
MR. WM. SCHUBERT,		MR. H. WORRELL.

All the newest styles of Brass and German-Silver Instruments constantly on hand, or made to order.

C. A. ZOEBISCH e HIJOS,
Importadores y Comerciantes por Mayor en
INSTRUMENTOS DE MUSICA, CUERDAS, &c.,
No. 46 Maiden Lane, Nueva York.
Depósito de las Célebres GUITARRAS de C. F. MARTIN y Ca., conocidas como las mejores del mundo.

Hemos recibido certificados de los tocadores siguientes, considerados los mejores que se conocen:—
La Señora de Goni, El Sr. de la Cova, El Sr. J. B. Coupa, El Sr. Chas. de Janon, El Sr. Wm. Schubert, El Sr. H. Worrell.
Se fabrican expresamente y se tienen siempre en almacen los mas modernos instrumentos de bronce y de plata alemana.

DRISCOLL & PALMER,
CARRIAGE GOODS,
No. 611 Broadway,
NEW YORK CITY, U. S.

We are prepared to fill all orders for MATERIALS for the MANUFACTURING of CARRIAGES, &c., and would solicit a call from Buyers, being satisfied they will find it to their interest to purchase their goods of us. Orders by Mail promptly attended to. Agents for WM. HARLAND & SONS' English Varnish and Japan.

DRISCOLL & PALMER,
NEGOCIANTES EN
Materiales para Carruajes,
No. 611 BROADWAY,
Ciudad de Nueva York, Estados Unidos.

Estamos preparados para desempeñar todas las órdenes que se nos dirijan relativas á la fabricacion de Carruajes, &c., y solicitamos una visita á nuestro establecimiento de parte de los compradores, quienes no dudamos encontrarán ventajoso el negociar con nosotros. Despacharemos en el acto toda órden recibida por el correo.
Agentes del Charol y Barniz Ingles de Wm. Harland & Sons.

THE NATIONAL STOVE WORKS,
239 & 241 Water St., New York,

Offer to Dealers a great variety of STOVES & HEATERS, manufactured at the founderies of the Company expressly for the trade.

The asortment includes various styles of COOKING STOVES of superior construction, strictly first-class, adapted to every want; also, Ranges, small Cooking Apparatus, and Hollow-ware. The stock includes a number of styles of **Heating Stoves and Furnaces** of greatly improved construction; also, the celebrated **Sanford's Challenge Hot-Air Furnace,** Portable, and set in Brick, with valuable improvements. A FIRE-PLACE HEATER is now in preparation, which will combine some special advantages.

Specimen Catalogues sent to all persons at their solicitation.

The following cuts represent a few of the leading styles.

Los grabados siguientes representan algunos de nuestros modelos.

BEACON LIGHT.
Portable Range. 4 Sizes.
BEACON LIGHT. Hornilla Portátcl. 4 tamaños.

MUTUAL FRIEND.
1st Class Cooking Stove. 4 Sizes.
MUTUAL FRIEND. Estufa de primera clase. 4 tamaños.

CONFIDENCE.
Cooking Stove. 4 Sizes.
CONFIDENCE. Cocina y Estufa. 4 tamaños.

Globe Heater. 5 Sizes.
Sandford's Mammoth, o Calentador de Globo. 5 tamaños.

Parlor Stove. 3 Sizes.
COSMOPOLITE. Estufa para salones. 3 tamaños.

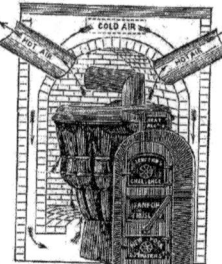
Portable. Set in Brick. Montado en ladrillo. 4 tamaños.
SANDFORD'S PATENT CHALLENGE HOT-AIR FURNACES. 3 Sizes.

GOOD WILL. Estufa y Cocina. 4 tamaños.

THE NATIONAL STOVE WORKS,
(LA FABRICA NACIONAL DE ESTUFAS,)
Nos. 239 y 241 Water Street, Nueva York.

Ofrece á los traficantes la mas extensa variedad de Estufas y Calentadores fabricados en las fundiciones de la Compañía, expresamente para el mercado.

El surtido incluye varios modelos de Cocinas de superior construccion, primera calidad, adaptadas a todas las necesidades, &c. Se enviara el Catálogo completo á todas las personas que lo soliciten.

BROOKLYN WHITE LEAD CO.,

Incorporated 1825.

MANUFACTURERS OF

White Lead, Red Lead and Litharge.

Trade Mark Label of Standard Brand.

CONSUMERS of Lead need be CAUTIONED that nine out of ten of the specious brands sold as Pure Lead are mere bogus productions.

Merchants, Manufacturers, Rail-Roads and Steam-Ships supplied with all grades of Lead, Dry or in Oil. Orders executed with promptness at lowest market rates.

1*st Quality Standard*—Blue Label; 2*d Quality* "*Refined*"—Yellow Label; 3*d Quality* "*Baltic*"—Red Label.

Business Address, 89 MAIDEN LANE, N. Y.

CARRIAGE CLOTHS.

Dusenbury & Ackerman,

IMPORTERS,

58 Murray Street, NEW YORK.

Constantly on hand at Lowest Market Rates, a full assortment of the best qualities of

CARRIAGE CLOTHS,

OF

English, French & German Manufacture,

Both in All

WOOL and UNION;

Also,

Silks,	Oil-Cloths,
Cotelines,	Buckrams,
Damasks,	Canvas,
Carpets,	Hair,

&c., &c., &c.

Quotations and Samples when Requested.

ABRAHAM R. VAN NEST,
FRANCIS A. THOMPSON,
ALEXANDER MURDOCH,
ALEXANDER T. VAN NEST.

Wholesale Saddlery & Coach Hardware,

A. R. VAN NEST & CO.

50 WARREN & 120 CHAMBERS STS.,

NEW YORK,

IMPORTERS AND MANUFACTURERS OF

Saddlery, Hardware, Harness Mountings

—AND—

CARRIAGE TRIMMINGS.

The Largest and most Complete Assortment of all descriptions of

Saddlery, Hardware, Harness & Carriage Goods,

Enameled and Patent Leathers,
Enameled Cloths and Oil-Cloths,
Broadcloths & Damasks of all Colors; Springs & Axles,
Carriage-Bolts and Carriage Wood-Work,
Every variety of Bits, Spurs, Stirrups, Bridles, &c.,
Harness-Buckles, Webs, &c.,
Horse Blankets & Sheets of every quality & description,
Lap-Robes and Afghans,

PARTICULAR ATTENTION GIVEN TO ORDERS SENT BY MAIL.

JOHN STEPHENSON & CO.,

No. 47 East Twenty-Seventh Street,

NEW YORK,

MANUFACTURE

STREET CARS

—AND—

OMNIBUSES

OF EVERY VARIETY.

This Establishment commenced building Street Cars in 1831, and is famed for Superior Elegance of Workmanship, and Substantial Practical Results.

Cyrus R. Crane & Co.

UPHOLSTERY

CARRIAGE, CAR,

AND

House Furnishing Dry Goods

56 WALKER, STREET, N.Y.

No. 2 Victoria Street, Manchester,

ENGLAND.

CYRUS R. CRANE,   LORIN P. CRANE.

BOUTON & SMITH,

77 & 79 Bowery, near Canal St., N. Y.

IMPORTERS & DEALERS IN

CARRIAGE HARDWARE,

Dry Goods, Wood Work, and Trimmings,

IRON AND STEEL.

Sole Agency for *LITTLEJOHN'S COMPOUND TIRE*, and *Farist's Celebrated Steel Tire.*

The Largest and Best Selected Stock of Materials, for all descriptions of Vehicles, in the U. S.

BOUTON, SMITH & CO.,
No. 185 GRAVIER STREET, NEW ORLEANS, LA.

BOUTON & SMITH,

Nos. 77 y 79 Bowery, cerca de Canal Street,

NUEVA YORK,

Importadores y Traficantes en Piezas de Hierro Madera para Carruajes y en todos los articulos necesarios para los mismos.

HIERRO Y ACERO.

Unicos Agentes del ESTAÑO COMPUESTO de LITTLEJOHN y de los Célebres AROS DE ACERO DE FARIST.

La coleccion mas extensa en los Estados Unidos de materiales para toda clase de Vehículos.

BOUTON & SMITH,
185 Gravier St., Nueva Orleans, La.

THE
Standard American Billiard Table.

This is the best and only reliable Billiard Table manufactured, and is furnished with our
IMPROVED COMBINATION CUSHION, PATENTED NOV. 26, 1867.

Besides having on hand Tables, Balls, Cloth, Cues, and every article appertaining to Billiards proper, we are manufacturing a

Table for the
HOME CIRCLE,
Patented, April 21, 1868.

Combining the Library Table, the Dining Table, and the Billiard Table.

For description and price, address

PHELAN & COLLENDER, Sole Patentees and Manufacturers,

Nos. 63, 65, 67, & 69 Crosby St., New York.

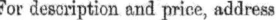

El Mejor Billar Americano.

Esta es la mejor Mesa de Billar y la única digna de crédito artre todas las que se fabrican va provista de muestras

Bombas mejoradas de combinacion, privilegiadas en 26 de Noviembre, 1867.

Ademas de tener siempre á mano Mesas, Bolas, Paño, Tacos, y todos los demas articulos relativos á Billares, fabricamos actualmente un

BILLAR DOMÉSTICO, privilegiado el 21 de Abríl, 1868.

Y que sirve à la voz de Mesa para Librería, para comer y para Jugar Billar.

Por descripciones y precios, ocùrrase á

PHELAN & COLLENDER, únicos fabricantes y dueños del privilegio,

Nos. 63, 65, 67, y 69 Crosby Street, Nueva York.

IMPORTACION DE DRAPERIAS, CORTINAS, VIDRIOSITE,

LOUIS WINDMÜLLER & ROELKER,

20 Reade Street, New York.

Importing Commission-Merchants
—AND—
MANUFACTURERS' AGENTS,

Upholstery and Curtain Goods,

Terrys, Brocatelles, Cotelines, Plushes,

BROADCLOTHS, DAMASKS, MOROCCO,

HAIR-SEATING,

WINDOW AND PICTURE GLASS,

GLASS FOR PHOTOGRAPHERS,

MADE BY

AUDRIS LAMBERT & CO., Marchienne au Paul.

☞ Orders with remittances or references promptly filled. Advances made on consignments of approved Merchandise.

Lightning Source UK Ltd.
Milton Keynes UK
UKHW050128170221
378876UK00013B/154